THE REAL POLICE

Stories from the Crescent City

James S. Prine

The Real Police

ISBN-13: 978-1547206100
ISBN-10: 1547206101

Back cover photograph of the author by
Deputy Dianna N. Becker, JPSO

First printing August 1996
Second printing January 1997
Second Edition, Third printing August 2017

REVIEWS

"Prineyman, James S. Prine, is the real deal. His eccentric, frank, intellectual yet radical presentation steps outside the bounds of normal police and literary recording. He delivers police emotions, and street survival techniques required to work 'the job' in a municipal environment that is more correctly compared to an urban jungle quagmire. If you wish to live, you almost have to abandon academy practices and learn the processes of the 'native thugs.' Remember, the animals of the jungle fear and respect ONE thing: FEAR. This book is an accurate account of the seriousness, the commitment and the humor of those who wear the badge in The Big Easy."

— Sergeant Roger C. Bull, Metro-New Orleans LEO.

"Jim Prine's "The Real Police" is the most true-to-life police book I've ever read. This book has been making the rounds of our unit, and the entire Police Department. Everyone who picks it up reacts in two ways...either they start grinning or they bust out laughing.

"Prine, who is a real cop, has taken a lot of heat for writing his book, but we admire him for having the he guts to go ahead and publish it.

"The stories are a faithful depiction of what actually happens in everyday police work. Frankly, I don't know how Prine got the other cops to talk to him about this stuff, or get permission to use their stories, but they are here for all to see. Good book, highly recommended if you like to read about actual cops and not Hollywood cardboard characters. To get any closer to the action, you'd have to swear the oath and pin on a badge yourself..."

—(Name withheld by request)

DEDICATION

This book is dedicated to the Disillusioned Warriors...

ACKNOWLEDGEMENTS

Many fine people made this book possible. The author wishes to express his thanks and appreciation to the following people. Without their encouragement, this book would still be nothing more than a collection of notes and audio tapes. Other individuals wished to remain anonymous, and I shall honor their wishes.

To my Mom and Dad: No one has ever been blessed with finer parents. Perhaps this book will, in some way, help you understand why I became a policeman, and, more importantly, why I stay in the profession. To my sister Debbie and my brother-in-law Guy Mitchell, for believing in me. To Daniel Paul Barker, my nephew, for his moral support and fine example. Dan is a poet and a warrior-priest, and we shall hear more about him some day.

To Dianna N. Becker, who has given me so much, and who honored herself and her family by becoming The Real Police. Joseph F. Revolta, Lisa, and Mrs. Ford, for their support, humor, and kindness while this book came into being.

Police Officer Eddie M. Eichaker and his wife Judy and daughter Asaya, who are fine people. Also: Detective Sergeant Gene Titman, Officer First Class John Leal, O.F.C. Dwayne Munch, Major Joseph J. Liquor, Jr., Homicide Detective Pascal Saladino (Retired), Senior Trooper George Lupo (Retired), Officer Ron Casse (Retired), Mr. Jose W. Cartagena, Mr. George Faulkner, Mr. Clyde Molero, Capt. Alan Abadie (Retired), Mr. Rusty Crawford, Capt. Larry Ingargiola, Sgt. Ben Glaudi, Detective O'Neil De Noux (Retired), Mrs. Lorraine Geyer, Father Warren Cooper, Lt. John Marie, Mr. Steve Geraci, Mr. Steve Collara, Special Agent Wayne Lee (Retired), Officer Steve Bulot

(Retired), Detective Sharon Moore, Capt. Alton J. Rachal, Mr. Harold Cathalougne, Sgt. Gilbert J. Mast (Deceased, Line of Duty), Lt. Brian Rainey, Sgt. Gavin Pagart, Officer Tommy Green, Officer Fred Conerly, Mr. Fred Yorsch, my Aunt Linda Prine, who, incidentally, bottles the finest pickles on the planet, and all my friends from Shoney's in Chalmette, many thanks are due.

Thanks to the dedicated and caring professionals of the Jefferson Parish Sheriff's Office, the City of Gretna Police Department, the Orleans Levee District Police Department, the St. Bernard Parish Sheriff's Department, Tulane's Department of Public Safety, the Louisiana State Police, and all my friends in other metro area law enforcement agencies. And, of course, my special thanks to my friends and colleagues in the New Orleans Police Department.

This is my second edition of "The Real Police." My manuscripts and books for the first edition were lost in Hurricane Katrina. Therefore, I'd like to acknowledge Sergeant Roger C. Bull, JPSO (retired) for skillfully retyping the files from a borrowed copy of my book. Roger is the Primary Member of Southern Oaks Publishing, LLC.

Sgt. Bull redesigned the book cover, along with Dea Meyer, the widow of Captain Don English, JPSO. Dea runs Hero-Ops, LLC. Her company designed and holds the copyright for the badge on the front cover.

INTRODUCTION

More policemen die by their own hand than die from criminal actions. That is not pleasant, but it is true. The night I wrote this introduction I watched a chilling reminder of that fact... video footage of a policeman that committed suicide in public, on camera, right in the middle of town. The policeman had killed his wife earlier in the day. His best friend, another policeman, actually had a long talk with him, and shook his hands before he pulled the trigger. He was saying goodbye to his friend and colleague, and both of them knew it. That happened in a small Louisiana town. Most policemen take a more subtle route to the grave; they drink or smoke too much, or they overeat. They work too much overtime. They pull too many details. Over the years, it takes its toll.

Many police deaths on duty are due to traffic accidents, either *en route* to a call or cut down in the street by what usually turns out to be a drunk driver. Relatively few policemen die or get crippled because of direct criminal action. On the other hand, during the writing of this book, I attended the funeral of a New Orleans Police Officer. Violence truly touches us all.

Policemen, by the very nature of their personalities and the constraints of officialdom, tend to internalize their stresses. That takes a terrible toll on the individual policeman. Many policemen develop drinking or drug abuse problems. The temptations of excitement and commitment-free sexual adventures take their toll on policemen and their families, too. Others succumb to the lure of quick money. One of the worst enemies of the policeman is Departmental politics and infighting. More policemen retire early because of 'bullshit burnout' than any other reason.

The world of a street policeman is a brutal reminder of the futility of human endeavor. The street policeman is immersed in despair, dirt, degradation and death. So we fight back, some more successfully than others. "Salvation is where you find it," say the street-preachers. They are right.

Humor quickly becomes one of the policeman's best allies. Often called 'sick' or 'gallows' humor, policemen try to lighten their load in the same way combat infantrymen do... they develop 'war stories.' On the following pages you will find a collection of 'war stories' from policemen in the New Orleans metro area. These stories were submitted by policemen from several agencies and many different assignments. Some of the events depicted occurred several years ago, and some were very recent. One of the delights in police work is its universal appeal; working street cops from all over the area will often find that they share similar experiences.

The format of this book is unusual in that there are no 'chapters' as such. I deliberately chose that approach in tribute to the irregularities of the street policeman's world... you never know what is next. So in these pages, you will see stories from NOPD and Gretna Policemen mixed in with tales from St. Bernard and JPSO (Jefferson Parish) Deputy Sheriffs. Detectives' stories will be mixed in with those of the infantry of the street policeman's world... the patrol officer.

So just pick up and start reading wherever you feel comfortable. I have included stories from every law enforcement agency in the New Orleans metropolitan area, where members would talk to me, a brother policeman. Also, included in the book are obscure facts about law enforcement and the New Orleans area. I had to leave some of the best stories out, for obvious reasons. Hopefully, you will get to share them in the future. You will also see memorable quotes after each story. You may feel that all the stories on these pages are incredible, or outright lies. That is your right.

The officers portrayed on these pages are actual people. Most of them are still engaged in law enforcement. Many of them have moved on to other departments or assignments, or retired from law enforcement duties. Some of them are dead. The names in this book were changed to preserve the privacy of the individuals involved, and for legal considerations.

You might feel, as I do, that most of them are heroes or heroines, as their gender dictates. Their courageous or devoted service should have been lauded but usually wasn't. Most of the material you see here was obtained from taped interviews (or "confessions') with individual Officers, or small groups of Officers. Any omissions or errors are the fault of the Author.

You will see that I use the term "policeman" or "policemen," instead of the more politically-correct term "police officer." That is deliberate. I did this not to demean female officers, but instead to pay tribute to the generations of policemen out there on the streets, whether their title was Deputy Sheriff, State Trooper, Detective, or Patrolman. It is only in the last few years that women have really entered street police work, so I use the term "policeman" as a mark of respect to the men that carried the badge and took the lumps before feminism entered the picture. On the memorial in front of NOPD Headquarters are the names of 94 Officers who have died in the line of duty, going back to 1890. All of the names belong to men.

Also, by "policeman," I refer to men and women actually engaged in street police duties, not administrative or ancillary personnel such as cooks or mechanics employed by a law enforcement agency. Lots of people carry badges, but most of them aren't *real police.*

My usage of the term "real police' refers to those cops who bring something special to law enforcement... be it a high standard of professionalism or technical expertise, compassion, or sheer humanity. Hopefully a real policeman has a mixture of all these traits. Humor, cynicism, and years of street experience all contribute to the making of a *real policeman.* A little craziness helps, too. Let me illustrate that point. An old story from the NOPD tells of a crazy man in the City who called his District station and told the desk Officer that he had an automatic rifle and thousands of rounds of ammunition, and was going to kill the first Policeman that showed up at his house. The eager NOPD cops wrecked two of their police cars, trying to be the first to confront the armed man. That is pure, 'Old Guard' NOPD, and that attitude still exists in some parts of the Department.

For any 'non-sworn persons' that have picked up this book, be forewarned that some of the events described on these pages are extraordinarily graphic. Several stories describe death scenes in graphic terms, and sexual activities also. *Real policemen* tend to have more than their share of testosterone, after all. The language is the language of the street. Please accept my apologies if the material does not meet your criterion for acceptable reading.

Why did I write this book? I didn't have any choice... I *had* to. The old boys are passing on, and their stories must be told. In fact, this book was originally meant for a 'police only' audience, but word of it leaked out and it has evolved into this glorious tome. In some ways, it is a story of my career in law enforcement as well. It took me many years of searching for the 'perfect' police agency before I finally realized that the 'ideal' agency doesn't exist... and it never will. I discovered that it doesn't really matter what department you work for, if you are sincere in your efforts to do the best job you can. Some of the finest of the *real police* work for small departments.

Part of being a policeman is hearing war stories from other cops, and experiencing the outer limits of reality yourself. These war stories help us maintain our sanity, and serve to give us insights into how other Officers handle their duties successfully. Good police work is an art. Policemen are *human beings*, and they have their share of human faults and virtues, just like everyone else. That will become very apparent on the following pages.

An old story from the Army paratroopers might put it in perspective. One day, a senior officer was inspecting a company of paratroopers. He asked them the usual questions. The officer came up to one young man, and asked him, "Soldier, how do you like jumping out of airplanes?" The young trooper blurted out the simple truth, "I hate it, Sir. It scares me to death!" The officer was amazed. He asked the young trooper, "Then what the Hell are you doing here in the Paratroopers, if you hate jumping out of airplanes?" The trooper answered him, truthfully, "Sir, I *like* serving with people who like jumping out of airplanes!" And so it is with *real policemen.*

I have made this solo Apache raid into a world of literary decency to bring you our stories, be they good or bad. You be the judge. Enjoy!

James S. Prine,
New Orleans, Louisiana
1996

CONTENTS

"HEADQUARTERS, 209 10-8."

"10-4, 209."

THE 64-T

"A long time ago I handled a '64-T.' Let me explain that one. I was down on patrol in my sector. Headquarters dispatched me to an armed robbery in Hopedale, a little place 'down the road.' One of my first! I was pretty excited, so I hurried to the address they gave me over the radio. I found my victim. He looked all right, so I immediately tried to get a description of the armed robber... This was *real* police work and I wanted to do everything just right.

"The victim told me the robbery had occurred a couple of hours earlier, and at that point, my enthusiasm began to ebb. I put a Code 4 over the radio so no one would get killed racing to *this* scene. I went to the patrol car and dug out my clipboard. I started getting the information for my police report. This was the story. It seems my victim, apparently a NASA reject, was down the road fishing miles from nowhere, all by himself. Or so he thought. Some man he had never seen before just appeared beside him, and told him hello.

"My victim, startled, just looked at the guy. Suddenly the stranger transformed himself into an armed robber. He produced a weapon, threatened the victim with it, and stole the victim's wallet. My victim, fearing for his safety, didn't resist, and the robber made good his escape.

"The weapon, by the way, was a *snapping turtle.* The robber had told the victim that he would make the turtle bite him if he didn't give up his wallet, so the damned fool just complied. The victim continued fishing a while, thinking about the robbery and how stupidly he had acted. He got angry, debated with himself about getting help, then finally scuttled his fishing expedition.

"He packed up his fishing gear, cranked up his old jalopy, and found a telephone. Presto, yours truly was launched to fight crime and evil. I think I only laughed openly at the victim a couple of times...when he described the 'weapon,' the damned thing had grown to what must have been a close cousin to Godzilla.

"Anyway, I got the information for the report and went back on patrol. The victim had only lost a few dollars and his cheapo plastic wallet; he didn't even *have* a driver's license so that was no problem. Let's just say I didn't run back to headquarters to put out a teletype or cut a bulletin. My Captain saw the report when I turned it in, and jumped on me instantly, scowling, for putting '64-T' in the signal box on the incident report, instead of the usual '64-G' (armed robbery with a gun) or '64-K' (armed robbery with a knife).

"I explained that the '64-T' referred to an armed robbery in which the weapon used was a turtle..." (Deputy Sheriff)

"To appreciate nonsense requires a serious interest in life."
(Gelett Burgess)

PARDON ME

"They put out a call about a house fire in my sector. I rolled over there, too. When I went 10-97, I saw smoke and flames issuing from the house. I radioed back that it was a real working fire, and that the house was fully involved, from what I could see. Excited neighbors told me that an old handicapped lady, who lived alone, was trapped inside. I could hear her yelling, too. One of the neighbors went off to get a key. She kept a spare key to the house for emergencies, but she just remembered that she had it.

"My rank came on the radio, asking about the situation, and I told him about the neighbor and the key. Later, he told me that he had authorized me to break in and rescue the lady, if the neighbor couldn't get there fast with the key. I guess in the excitement and confusion, all I understood was the order to 'break in.' Put it down to auditory blocking. So anyway, I *did* break in... I smacked my size thirteen right into the door. It popped open instantly. No problem getting that door open.

"What *was* the problem was that the old lady, up against the door with her walker, got nailed square in the forehead with the doorknob when I smashed the door in. POW! She and her walker flew across the room. I thought I'd killed her..., but I went in there and scooped her up and took her outside, into the fresh air, and away from the fire.

"Our EMS guys and the Fire Department people were just arriving while I was getting her outside. The old lady was all right, but boy, did I put a big knot on her head." (Police Officer)

"I'm not against the police; I'm just afraid of them."
(Alfred Hitchcock)

THE CATCHBACK

"All *real policemen* like practical jokes, and they *love* catch-backs. This other deputy, Tony, had offended me in a practical joke, so I wanted to get even with him. I discussed this with my partner. Both of us are sadistic bastards, so we cooked up a good one.

"Tony had a take-home police car that he proudly parked in front of his house. His car was the key to the catch-back.

"While he was off duty and safely asleep, my partner and I 'slim-jimmed' our way into his car and planted incriminating evidence in it, for his wife Lisa to find. Lisa's reputation for jealousy was legendary, as was her temper.

"We put an obviously used set of lacy panties and bra in the car, some lipstick-stained Kleenex, and cigarette butts in the ashtray...the whole works. All these goodies had been obtained from a female accomplice.

"We planted the incriminating items carefully so they couldn't be *too* obvious. I even had an opened condom package that I placed carefully under Tony's side of the front seat...you could just glimpse a corner of it, if you looked that way. Perfect! I squirted some cheap perfume into the car, to add the finishing touch. My giggling partner and I skulked away.

"A couple of hours later, we called Tony's house from another house up the street. Lisa answered the phone. I asked to speak to Tony, but Lisa told me he was asleep. I had counted on that, of course. I shot the breeze with her a minute or so, then asked her to see if Tony had brought my Sheriff's Office jacket into the house. I told her that he had picked it up for me at a crime scene, and I needed it for a detail. She told me it was probably still in Tony's car, because he hadn't brought it into the house. I asked Lisa to check his car; and that, if she found it, I'd come right over and pick it up. Lisa told me to hang on while she went out and checked the car.

"We hurried to the window, stifling our giggles. We had set up a spotting 'scope to see her reaction when she found the 'evidence.' Lisa walked out the front door, walked innocently to the Sheriff's Office car, unlocked it, and opened the door. The scent of the perfume must have hit her then...we saw her dive into the car, examining the goodies we had planted for her to find.

"BINGO!

"Lisa jerked herself out of the car, holding the lacy panties aloft and waving them like a trophy as she ran back into the house, yelling like a maniac...

"We could hear her yells from *our* position down the block! I hurried back and grabbed the phone so I could enjoy the sound effects. I could hear her screaming, "You sonofabitch! You screwed her in the police car, you rotten bastard!"

"Then we heard Tony's bewildered denials as she attacked poor Tony and beat the shit out of him.

"I put the phone quietly back on the hook. My grinning, evil smirk told my co-conspirators that we had pulled it off. We went right over to Tony's house pronto and patched up the situation...

"Tony had an already-swelling eye where Lisa had popped him a good lick. Lisa eventually forgave us, but Tony swore vengeance. He got it, too. *Those* were the good old days... " (Deputy Sheriff).

> *"Human salvation lies in the hands of the creatively maladjusted."*
>
> *(Dr. Martin Luther King)*

LANDSHARK

"Joe and I assassinated a dog one night. This dog had been pestering us for a while. One night it made the fatal error of biting

Joe, lightly, on one leg. Enough! The dog had to go. We wanted to just *shoot* the sonofabitch, but we couldn't have witnesses seeing their police blowing away a dog. So we scooped up the dog and took it to the normal place of execution, Paris Road, out by Bayou Bienvenue.

"We had to Alpo® that dog into the police car...we used dog food to coax him in so we could capture him. The mutt settled down and enjoyed what would happen to be *his* last supper. We drove him out to Paris Road; traffic was light, because it was *very* late.

"Joe, always properly outfitted for the task at hand, stoked up his little Ruger .22 revolver, his favorite death weapon, with hollow-point .22 Long Rifle cartridges. I would be his back-up, with my Colt .45 automatic pistol. We chose a good spot on the old road. It was very dark and right up against the bayou. No traffic. The denizens of the swamp would make short work of the dog's carcass after we'd snuffed out its life.

"We discussed the plan...I would grab the dog and toss him out into the waters of the bayou, and Joe would blast him with the .22, killing him. The dog would sink into the dark water...no muss, no fuss. The crabs, shrimp, and other swamp creatures would take care of the rest. An excellent plan. We put it into play...

"After making certain no witnesses could see our deed, I snatched the dog out of the police car and carried him over to the shoreline of the swamp. Joe hefted the .22 and assumed a firing stance. The dog *knew* he was dead meat, then...he must have sensed it. He went nuts, wriggling around and trying to bite me, but I was ready for him. Joe said, "Now!" I tossed the struggling mutt out into the swamp.

"Joe started firing at the beast as it splashed into the water.

He was fanning the hammer of the little single-action revolver, cowboy style. He really had it popping away....those vicious little .22 slugs were really chewing up that dog. I stepped further and further back, away from Joe and the screaming dog.

"Trouble was, the dog *wasn't* following our plan! That damned dog absorbed the.22 bullets with no effect. Somehow, it *charged* back at us, seemingly running on the surface of the water, as it streaked back at Joe, howling and barking, plainly insane in its pain and rage. Its eyes were slits. It looked like it was *all teeth* as it came on. Joe, the empty .22 hanging uselessly at his side, stared in amazement as the dog charged him in its death run.

"Joe spoke in a chant, gradually increasing his volume as the dog neared..."*He's gonna get me!... He's gonna GET ME!"* Truly realizing that the dog *was* going to get him, Joe started backpedaling, faster and faster, toward me. Joe looked at me, stunned, and then glanced back at the rampaging dog.

"He said, in an incredulous voice, "*He's really gonna GET ME!"* The yowling dog hit him then, low in the leg, chewing earnestly and growling deeply as it gnawed Joe's leg...the one it *hadn't* bitten before!

"Joe screamed, *"HE'S GETTING ME! HE'S GETTING ME!"* as he tried to shake off the kamikaze dog, who was *really* working his leg over. Joe had dropped the little Ruger and was trying to pull the dog off with both hands as he danced up and down, screaming *"HE'S GETTING ME!"*

Me, the trusted back up, what was *I* doing as the dog was eating Joe's leg? Hell, I was doubled over, laughing my *guts* out...I was really enjoying the spectacle! Nothing against Joe, but it was just too funny. I didn't know Joe could dance like that! Then, things turned serious...Joe managed to get the maniac dog off his thoroughly chewed leg, and the damned thing came for *me.* It wasn't funny anymore. I guess the sonofabitch wanted a couple of bleeding cops to brag about.

"I stopped laughing and pulled my .45, snapping off the thumb safety as the bloody, still energetic dog made a fast pass at my leg. I stepped back smartly as the dog lunged, and fired straight down into the top of his head. POW! The dog crumbled instantly and died, the big .45 slug doing its job most satisfactorily. I reholstered the pistol after putting the thumb safety back on, reached down, grabbed the inert dog, and heaved him out into the swamp. He didn't come back *this* time.

"Joe, starting to *really* hurt now, raised Hell with me because I had let the dog 'get' him. I started laughing again, which really got him upset. The dog had ripped impressive holes in Joe's uniform pants and his leg.

"We went back in, and I patched Joe up. Soon, the incident became yet another humorous war story. We called that dog the 'Land Shark'..." (Sergeant)

"Everything is funny as long as it is happening to somebody else."
(Will Rogers)

THE CARJACKING

"We'd been sent to (name deleted) Hospital to investigate a 34-S (shooting) victim who had survived an attempted carjacking. We'd been notified by the hospital authorities, because of the gunshot wound. It was in fact a minor wound, but they were required by State law to report all gunshot injuries to the police, meaning us.

"We met the victim in the Emergency Room and asked him where his car was...we needed to get the Crime Lab out, to check it over and obtain any physical evidence available. The victim, a prosperous-looking white male in his mid-fifties, stunned us when he told us it was parked out in the parking lot. He'd just parked it out in the regular parking lot, like he was visiting someone. This made me curious. If I'd just survived a carjacking attempt and getting shot in the gut, I don't think I'd take the time to park my car like that. He was just a little too cool, if you know what I mean. It just didn't sound normal.

"We started getting some information from the victim, trying to get a handle on what had actually happened. The victim just didn't seem sincere. I smelled a rat. My partner stayed with him, carefully taking his statement while I got a description of his car and went outside to examine it. I found the car parked out in the visitor's parking lot. I looked it over..., a late-model four-door sedan, a plush luxury model... really nice. When I looked inside, I *knew* the guy was full of crap. The seat belts, on the rear seat, were neatly arranged. There was no evidence whatever of a desperate fight in *that* car. It was pristine. He'd even cleaned the blood off the leather seat where he was supposedly 'shot.' No way was I buying *this* story.

"I returned while my partner was still getting information from the 'victim.' The guy said he was driving back from one of the Gulf Coast casinos. He'd stopped on the Interstate (I-10) to pick up four white male hitch-hikers, all strangers to him, who said they were going to New Orleans. When they got to New Orleans, a couple of miles from the Paris Road exit, the four men attempted to carjack him. He said one of them had pulled a gun on him. They beat him and shot him, when he fought back.

Amazingly, he kept fighting and managed to get them all out of the car. He left them out there, on the Interstate. The victim told us he couldn't identify any of the men, but he had a hunch they were from Chalmette, because they were white and looked 'kinda scruffy' by his standards.

"At that point I broke in, "That is a very interesting story, and it is total bullshit, Mister. I do believe you were over on the Gulf Coast, but I bet you were with a woman. Am I right?" I asked him. When he put his head down, I *knew* we had him. He nodded silently.

"And *she* shot you, right?" I asked. He nodded again.

"I went on, "... and I bet she wasn't your wife. Am I correct, sir?" Another sheepish nod.

"I asked him quietly, "You want to try another bullshit story on us, or do you want to talk to some cops over there in Mississippi, where this actually happened?"

"He looked up at me, red-faced. "Can I think it over for a while, Officer?" I just looked over at my partner and grinned..." (Police Officer)

"To know all is not to forgive all. It is to despise everybody."
(Quentin Crisp)

THE UFO

"One night they dispatched a call about a UFO in Parc Chenier (now Sidney Torres Park). It was one of those cold, foggy nights. Nothing much was going on. The idea of a flying saucer amused me, so I rolled over there, too. There *was* a red light in the fog, flashing at irregular intervals. It was weird. I went 10-97 on the radio and another patrol unit pulled up. We all got out with our flashlights and approached the 'UFO' to see what it was.

"It turned out to be a couple of kids in a car. They'd had a school function that evening and managed to wind up in the back of Parc Chenier where it was cozy and dark. They thought nobody'd bother them. They were screwing their brains out, of course, and didn't notice our approach. The other deputies looked at me. I nodded, stepped forward, and tapped on the windshield with my Kel-Lite.

"Both of them came, eh, 'unglued.' I had to chuckle; the boy hadn't even bothered removing his tuxedo jacket. I told them, "Police! Look, I know what you're doing out there, and I'm not your Momma or your Daddy, so it doesn't bother me, kids. But I'm afraid you can't do that stuff out here in the park. You might get hurt. We might have been bad guys instead of cops. Go someplace else. Go get a motel room or something, or just get out of the Parish. Have a nice night."

"The boy, flustered, trying desperately to get his clothes together, asked me how we'd spotted them out there in the darkness. I spelled it out for him. "Next time you're getting some nooky in a car, kid, keep your foot off the brake pedal!" (Deputy Sheriff)

"Remember that something being legal doesn't necessarily make it right..."

(Old saying)

COULDN'T WAIT

"One night, I was patrolling northbound on Louisiana 47 (Paris Road). Some guy came along, flying low. He blew my doors off! I snapped on the emergency lights and siren, and started flashing my high beams to get the driver's attention. I wanted to stop him from killing himself, driving like that.

"The driver, a man, just waved his hand out his window in a lazy motion. I got right on his ass, blasting with the siren and flashing my headlights in his mirror, but the guy would just give me the little wave. I was furious. I kicked in a 10-28 (Request for emergency radio clearance). I announced that I was in hot pursuit northbound on Paris Road...I gave a description of the vehicle, the license plate, and all that, according to policy.

"I really wanted to catch the guy. It had become a personal matter. Just before the big green bridge, he finally pulled over, by the Gulf Outlet. I hopped out of the car and ran up to him, as the driver emerged with his license and registration already in hand. He said, "I know, Officer. I was really driving fast, but I was, er, 'occupied.' My wife said she couldn't wait to get me home, so she was giving me an emergency blowjob. I'm sorry."

"I looked into the car, and his wife was nodding enthusiastically. "Yes sir, Officer, he's telling the truth," she said, "I just couldn't wait to get him."

"I put out a Code 4 (no other units needed) and just let them go, shaking my head. No one would believe this crap anyway..." (Deputy Sheriff)

Interpol (International Criminal Police Organization) was

formed in Vienna in 1923.

MARDI GRAS RENDEZVOUS

"I'd only been out of the NOPD Academy a short time...just a few months. We were getting ready for Mardi Gras. The old timers were telling us rookies all sorts of war stories about Mardi Gras. One guy kept telling us how you could turn a pair of beads into a blow job, if you could handle yourself right. Crazy women, usually very drunk, would show their boobs for a pair of Mardi Gras beads or maybe a doubloon, or a lot more, if they were drunk or crazy enough. He told us people *came* to New Orleans to be crazy and get drunk and screw strangers. They came from all over the world to have wild fun here. How right he was...

"Anyway, I was working a barricade for a night parade. I was stationed at the corner of St. Charles Avenue at Julia, a pretty good location. I was having a good time, really enjoying myself; and, somehow, I started talking to this little chick from Ohio.

"She was *nice*, if you know what I mean...*very* well-developed, no bra. She was wearing a fishnet blouse that left nothing much to the imagination. She was pretty and had a good personality, so we really hit it off.

"I started giving her the Mardi Gras junk that came my way. The krewes really throw lots of shit at the police. Most of it is worth keeping, but I gave my goodies to her. Beads, doubloons, panties, plastic cups, spears, T-shirts, you name it. What the Hell. I'm a bachelor, and I don't collect that stuff anyway. The young lady's boyfriend saw that we were getting pretty friendly. He wasn't *that* drunk, but I didn't care much about him. If he had become an asshole, I'd just handle up on him, you know what I mean?

"The girl had been having her fair share of beers and other drinks, too. Eventually, she had to pee. She didn't know where to go, but I helped her out. I'm a nice guy. I took her over to the Sewerage and Water Board building. I had the girl by the hand and gave the security guard a bullshit story about how she was my wife. She really needed to go in and use the restroom, she was about to pop. The guard let us in, and the girl went into the ladies' room and did her business. I waited outside, like a good cop.

"She called out to me to come in and help her. She was 'having problems,' as she put it. I went into the restroom, and of course, she was stark raving naked. And giggling. That girl *was* really fine. Anyway, she raped me, but I wasn't in any mood to press charges. A certain portion of my anatomy had dry heaves, though, if you know what I mean. She really tore my ass up.

"Later, we got back to my post. Her boyfriend was staring daggers at me. He *knew* we'd been up to some hanky-panky.

"My Sergeant came by later and said to me, "You asshole. What kind of example do you think you make? People expect a New Orleans Police Officer to be something *special.* You're a disgrace to the Department...," then he winked. He was a real policeman. He knew what had happened. All the cops out there knew I'd gotten my pipes cleaned, and they just ate it up." (Police Officer)

"Love is not the dying moans of a distant violin .It's the triumphant twang of a bedspring."

(S.J. Perelman)

BLOODSPRAY

"We had this Irish cop riding along with us, over here observing American police techniques. Our police car was a piece of shit. As a matter of fact, the first day he rode with us it broke down. We had to put in a new starter. We did the work ourselves, which really seemed to impress the Irish dude. Anyway, we got involved in a Signal 30, a homicide, out near Venetian Isles, the good old Seventh District. Actually, it was first put out as a 103 (fight). We rolled out there, a fifteen or twenty-minute ride. On the way, the 103 turn into a 94-S (gunshots), so we rolled faster. Then the 94-S turned into a 34-S (someone shot), so we went the rest of the way on a Code 3 (lights and sirens).

"When we got there, it was a Signal 30. We saw this hysterical woman running around in the street. When she saw the police car, she ran up to us, crying. She told us that she'd just shot her ex-boyfriend. We checked her for weapons, but she was clean. We walked over to the scene of the shooting, a little two-level apartment complex. On the way, my partner asked her how long he had been an 'ex' boyfriend. The woman told us since today. He'd been beating the shit out of her, and she had had enough of it. She borrowed a revolver to protect herself.

"Today, he came over, screamed at her, and was attempting to force his way into her apartment when she picked up the gun and told him to go away. He laughed at her and started kicking in the door when she panicked and popped off a shot next to the door, to scare him off.

"The .38 Special bullet went through the wall and hit the 'ex-boyfriend' in the eye and killed him instantly. It was the bloodiest mess you could imagine. I was hoping the Irish cop would be impressed with our southern hospitality, but he said he was used to bloody bodies back in Ireland. We believed him. Blood was pooled up below the 'ex-boyfriend' and was dripping down the stairs. Huge amounts of blood. Unfortunately, there was this big air-conditioning unit under the stairs. Its fan was running. The blood was dripping onto the fan, which flung it out onto the walls. It made this pretty design on the wall that you wouldn't believe. We couldn't turn the fan off. It just kept making this fancy design on the wall..." (Police Officer)

"I hasten to laugh at everything for fear of being obliged to weep at it."

(Pierre de Beaumarchais)

FAST FOOD

"I was on patrol and proceeding through an intersection, when this idiot came barreling through the red light and damned near got me. I was shocked. It was *so* close. I was in a marked patrol car and everything. I switched on the emergency overhead lights and siren, and went after the guy. It took him forever to slow down and pull over. When he finally got his car stopped, he got out with a funny look on his face, like he was embarrassed. I put out a Code 4 and approached the driver. I started chewing his ass for nearly hitting me at the intersection. He asked me to just look into his car, and I'd see why he'd run the light. I did go over and look into the car. His wife was sitting in there with this huge pot of red beans and rice on her lap, steaming hot. That pot was brimming, too. If the driver had hit the brakes it would have spilled all over the place and burned her legs. I just shook my head and let them go." (Deputy Sheriff)

"Ordinarily he was insane, but he had lucid moments when he was

merely stupid."

(Heinrich Heine)

ATTITUDE

"I handled a Signal 20 (automobile accident) out on Lakeshore Drive near the U.N.O. campus. You know the kind, just property damage, no injuries. Take the information and file the report. No big deal. Well, the kid that initiated the accident was a U.N.O. student with a real attitude problem. A wise-ass. I wrote the accident and issued him citations for failure to maintain control, no proof of insurance, and the like, nothing special. But, he was going to cough up some bucks to the City.

"The kid flipped out. He started making noises about my *quota* and shit like that. What an idiot. We don't *have* quotas, we can write as many citations as we want. But he sort of got under my skin, so I got him away from the other people.

"I got in *his* face, and told him, "Look, kid, you're a college student. That means you're here to learn things. You don't know it all yet, so just shut up. One day, if you graduate from this place, and live long enough, then maybe you'll know it all. *Then* you can be a cop, like me, and know *everything."*

"He looked at me for a second, then absolutely broke up. He *loved* it. He signed his tickets, and I cut him loose..." (Police Officer)

"Justice is my being allowed to do whatever I like.Injustice is whatever prevents my doing so."

(Samuel Butler)

RAIN

"I was raised on TV and movies. I thought I knew everything there was about guns and gunfights. Hell, I grew up with this stuff since I was a little kid. You know, on television, the bad guy takes a couple of rounds in the chest, and they make little red spots on his shirt. Time for a commercial. No big deal at all.

"I got to handle a 29-S (suicide) my second day on the job. Some dude stuck a 12-gauge shotgun in his mouth and fired it with a stick pressed against the trigger. Lucky us get the call. We went 10-97 about five minutes after this guy blew his brains out. We walked into his apartment, past the onlookers and freaked-out neighbors and other people milling around running their heads, squawking and yammering about how terrible it was...

"It was *unreal*. The guy's head had literally exploded. I mean, there was goo *everywhere,* on every surface. It was un-fucking-be*lievable.* It looked like the guy had spray-painted his apartment, and in a sense, he had. Stuff was dripping off the ceiling. It was literally raining brains and stuff off the ceiling. The sight and smell of it made me nauseated, but I handled it. But that scene sure made me revise my opinion of what gunfire could do to the human body." (Police Officer)

> *The world's first modern, metropolitan police department was formed in the City of London, England, in 1829. It was then, and is now, called the Metropolitan Police. Its founder was Sir Robert Peel (1788-1850), and people still call London Police Officers "Bobbies," and at one time they were also referred to as "Peelers."*

HE DIED WITH HIS BOOTS ON

"We got a signal 29 (death) up on St. Claude, in Arabi. A dead man found in his own car. Nude, except for his cowboy boots. He was spotted in the morning by passers-by. Later, one of the detectives gave me the story. The dead guy had picked up a prostitute in New Orleans and took her back to Arabi to do the deed. She literally fucked him to death. He died of a massive heart attack.

"The grinning detective added that the guy 'came and went at the same time'. But I had the last word. I told him, "Yeah, but, at least, he died with his boots on!" The detective just cracked up. (Deputy Sheriff)

"Cities, like cats, will reveal themselves at night."
(Rupert Brooke)

SHOPLIFTER

"My partner, Bobby, was working an off-duty detail at a convenience store on Magazine Street. This store clerk came up to him, all excited, and pointed out a woman. The clerk told Bobby that she had seen the woman shoplifting a blood pressure kit...a box containing a blood-pressure cuff, a stethoscope, and the packaging. The woman had been seen shoving the kit up her dress, between her legs. Bobby went over to the women, told her what was going on, and escorted her discreetly back to the Manager's office. Bobby told her that one of the clerks had seen her take the merchandise, and where she had put it. As it turned out, the shoplifter, wearing a long dress, was a bitch with an attitude.

"She shrilly denied taking the kit, at the top of her voice, and told Bobby that she had just put some tissue paper up between her legs because she was on her period. She actually reached down between her legs and pulled out some bloody tissue paper. This pissed Bobby off, because she deliberately tried to gross him out. She was insulting his intelligence and crapping on his badge.

"Bobby told her, "Lady, we can do this easy or hard. You can pull out the merchandise and get out of here. Or, you can play asshole, and I'll get a female Officer over here to get it. Or, I can haul your ass to Central Lockup, and *they* can get it for me. Make up your mind, and don't take all day." The woman nodded silently, very pissed off, but getting the best of the deal, and she knew it. She reached in and took out the bloody, nasty kit. Bobby chewed her ass but then cut her loose.

"The store Manager got upset and asked Bobby why the woman wasn't going to jail. Bobby told him the score. "Hey, Mister, do you really think I'm going to get up there in Court and testify to what she just did? Not hardly." In the end, the store Manager discarded the soiled kit and chalked it off to experience. (Police Officer)

"Thieves respect property. They merely wish the property to become their property that they may more perfectly respect it." (G. K. Chesterson)

HER FAULT

"I remember one time, we were going Code 3 to a call, and this dog was chasing a cat up the street. My partner, Eddie, who was driving, said, "Damn, look at that dog chasing that cat. I hope he doesn't run out in the street." Sure enough, the cat shot across the street, but the stupid dog didn't make it. We heard a little 'clunk, clunk' underneath the car, right, but continued to our call. Later we came back, intending to get the dog's body out of the street, call Sanitation to come out, and pick it up.

"Well, we handled the call, but when we got back, the dog was gone! We were *highly* impressed, because we *knew* we'd really nailed him good. We'd figured he was hamburger meat. What had really happened was that the dog's owner had seen the whole incident, came outside, and picked up her dog. She dragged it to the side of the street. Its insides were crushed, and it was dying. The owner, a little old lady, was there with her dog, crying, trying to give water to her dying dog and comfort it. I felt terrible.

"What does Eddie do? He puts the liability on *her*. He asked her, "Why wasn't your dog on a leash? Do you know I could write you a ticket for that? Your dog could have caused an accident, and you'd be responsible!" He put the whole responsibility on *her*, so typically NOPD." (Police Officer)

"The welfare of the people is the greatest law." (Cicero)

BAG MAN

"We had this guy on St. Charles Avenue. He was going to commit suicide by jumping out of one of those hotels. He was drunk and despondent and was going to kill himself by jumping from a window fifteen stories up. I'd never see anyone die from splattering on a city street, so I coaxed my partner, Gene, to go over there so I could get this experience. When we got to the scene, I saw a fire department guy, so I walked over to him and tried to talk to him.

"I said, "Hey, Cap, what are you guys going to do on a

thing like this? Y'all got one of those big air bag things that you lay out in the street and inflate, so the guy will survive if he decides to jump?"

"The fire department guy looked at me like I was a complete moron, then he grinned and said,"'Man, are you for real? This is New Orleans. We haven't got any shit like that!" He went on, "And, the bag we *do* have won't do him any good above four floors, anyway. If that asshole jumps, I just hope he doesn't land on us or one of our vehicles...his ass is toast."

"I asked him, 'Then why is the fire department out here, if you guys can't help him?"

"The fireman shrugged his shoulders, shook his head, and said, 'I don't know, buddy, but some idiot called the fire department, though, and here we are." (Police Officer).

The first metropolitan police department in the United States was formed in New York City in 1844.

THE DRIVE IN

"I was off duty and watching a movie at the St. Bernard drive-in. Now, this place had a traffic control device at the exit, one of those treadle plates. Spikes, spring-loaded, so you could drive over them safely in one direction; but, if you drove over them the other way, the points punctured your tires. No one watched the exit, and it was pretty dark back there.

"Now, some people, hoping to save a little money, would place a sheet of plywood or a board over the spikes and drive in without paying. This particular time, I was parked near the exit, and suddenly heard a lot of noise and commotion. I decided to check it out, so I walked back there to see what was going on.

"Dumb assholes blew all four tires on their car! Their driver believed that if he *backed* over the spikes fast they wouldn't have any effect on his tires. WRONG! I laughed my ass off." (Deputy Sheriff).

"You can beat the rap, but you can't beat the ride..."
(Detective)

DOG BITE

"We got a call one day... a Signal 21 (complaint) in reference to a dog bite. I was elated; this involved no paperwork for us. it was just a civil matter. We got to the address they gave us and saw a little girl bleeding heavily from her side. I said to myself, *"Aw shit!"* This was a *bad* dog bite she'd received. This *was* some paperwork after all. We got an ambulance rolling on a Code 3, because of the heavy bleeding. We started talking to neighbors, to see what had happened, and to find out where the dog was. We had to make sure it couldn't bite anyone else.

"They said that at the corner of Wales and, I think, it was Mercier Street a small group of kids were walking along in the street. A big pit bull dog came out from underneath a car and charged the kids. It grabbed the little girl, knocked her down and began chewing her up. A man with a shovel came along, alerted by the girl's screaming, and cracked the dog on the head, beating it. He managed to get the dog off the girl and he chased the dog into a yard with a hole in the fence. Apparently it was where the dog had escaped from. The man rolled an empty 55-gallon steel drum in front of the hole, so the dog couldn't get out, then he called us.

"We let the man lead us back to the yard with the dog. When I first saw the dog I said, *"Damn! That is one big dog!"* We called out the SPCA. While we were waiting for them to arrive, I examined the dog and the hole in the fence. I realized that the dog had made the hole with his *teeth.* I was *impressed.* I said to my partner, "Now, that is one serious puppy. What kind of dog could chew out a section of chain-link fence with his *teeth?"*

"We tried to get the people at the house to open up, but we couldn't get any response. We notified our rank, advised her of what was going on, and told her that the ambulance had taken the girl to (name deleted) Hospital for treatment. We were just waiting for the SPCA people to come get the dog, so we could clear the scene and write up the report. No problem.

"When the SPCA guy arrived, he checked out the dog and announced that he'd just snare him. He asked if we could help him open the gate and ease the dog into the truck. That was fine with us. The dog, feeling his territory violated, started getting weird and acting up.

"When the SPCA man tried to snare the dog, it snatched that snare and tugged on it, hard It jerked the SPCA man through the gate. We were *impressed!* We had a lot of respect for that dog, pulling a full-grown man through the gate like that.

"We helped get the SPCA man's snare away from the dog, and watched the SPCA man make another attempt. It was successful. We opened the gate so the SPCA man could ease the dog out of the yard and over to the truck. The dog was fighting it, big time. At one point, the SPCA man jerked on the snare, apparently to get the dog into a better position. Something went wrong, and the snare snapped. The gate opened, and the dog came out...fast.

"My partner George started backing slowly. I did the same, unsnapping my holster and pulling my Beretta pistol. The dog got down in a crouching position, preparing to spring onto the SPCA man. As the dog made the first forward movement, I shot him twice with the nine-millimeter Beretta. The first bullet tore up his chest cavity. The second one fragmented in his mouth, with particles entering his skull. But, at that instant, the shots had absolutely no effect on the dog.

"Abruptly, it suddenly relaxed and walked back into the yard, away from the SPCA man, and us. George started laughing, a nervous laugh. Then he got on the radio and called the rank, telling them we had a 30 (homicide) on a dog. He tried to get Homicide out. He was calling *everybody* out. He embarrassed me immensely. A shitload of paperwork and other bullshit followed. (Police Officer)

"Who is the real police? I'll tell you... a real policeman has the knack for doing the right thing at the right time, for the right reason. Consistently. And not getting caught doing it. What constitutes 'right' depends upon the situation, and the policeman's maturity, experience, judgment, training,and available resources. That is situational ethics at its ultimate. That is life on the street. You learn to deal with the street, or it will certainly deal with you."

(Author)

SHOOT HIM!

"A couple of days after I shot the pit bull, we got flagged

down at the corner of Dwyer and Wright Road. There was a large group of people clustered around, looking down into the canal. We pulled over to see what it was. I was thinking to myself, *"Shit, here we go again. A 30. Somebody got shot and they dumped the body here in the canal..."*

"I got out to get a look at whatever was in the canal. Then I saw... a monster alligator. It must have been ten or twelve feet long! I called it in over the radio, telling the dispatcher that we were out with a Signal 21. We gave her the location. The dispatcher wanted to know what the '21' was in reference to, so like an idiot I told her...a big alligator in the canal. What did the clowns in the District start saying, when they heard me put it out? "SHOOT HIM! SHOOT HIM!" . (Police Officer)

> *"It is vain to say human beings ought to be satisfied with tranquility; they must have action; and they will make it if they cannot find it."*
>
> *(George Eliot)*

I'M STILL AFLOAT

"Late one night we got a Signal 20-I (accident with injury) on St. Bernard Highway in Arabi, near Center Street. Where the canal is, right next to the railroad tracks. A driver had been speeding into New Orleans and lost control. We got to the scene pretty fast, but had to look around for the driver; he'd been ejected from his vehicle.

"I wandered around and finally found the driver in the canal, in about eight or ten inches of cold, muddy water. He was extremely drunk, but not too badly banged up. I sloshed over to the guy and checked him out. As I examined him, I asked him how he was doing. The asshole told me, "Don't worry about me, pal... I'm still afloat!" Turned out he was in the Coast Guard. I still smile when I pass that spot. (Deputy Sheriff)

"Wine makes a man better pleased with himself; I do not say that it makes him more pleasing to others."

(Dr. Samuel Johnson)

THE BATTLE OF ARABI

"You ever heard of the Battle of Arabi? It was the proudest moment in the history of the St. Bernard Sheriff's Office. This happened a long time ago, but it's worth repeating.

"There were these two old coots that used to work the day watch in Arabi. They spent a lot of time in the Royal Castle hamburger place on St. Claude Avenue, at the corner of LeBeau Street. The place itself is gone now, they tore it down years ago.

"But, let me get back to the story. These two old Deputies were inside the Royal Castle, drinking coffee and shooting the breeze with their cronies, you know? They had left their police car outside, parked partially on the sidewalk. Its keys were in the ignition, since nothing ever happened in Arabi, anyway, back in those days.

"A punk kid came along and looked the police car over. It intrigued him. The kid wanted to take it for a joy ride. So he went ahead and did it. He jumped into the car, started it, and took off, laughing like a fool.

"Inside the Royal Castle, one of the deputies heard the car

start up, and, when it pulled off, he jumped off his stool and ran outside to stop the kid and retrieve his police car!

"The kid accelerated westbound on St. Claude, laughing at the old deputy, who flipped out and went for his gun. Yessir! The deputy yanked out his old .38 and yelled something like, "Stop, police" or some crap like that. The kid kept going, even faster.

"Finally, in desperation, the old deputy blasted off a round. POW! Straight up, as a warning shot. Unfortunately, he was directly underneath a street light, one of those big old thick, heavy, frosted-glass globes with the light bulb inside.

"It exploded, shattered all to hell. The pieces rained down and hit the deputy below. Boy, did they hit him. He fell down on the sidewalk, knocked senseless and cut with the falling glass and blood everywhere. Knocked him cold.

"By this time, the *other* deputy finally got outside and spotted his partner lying bloody and unresponsive on the sidewalk. The gunshot and the exploding street light had him excited enough already. But when he saw his buddy there on the sidewalk, apparently gunned down, he went berserk! He figured the asshole in the car... *his* car, had shot his buddy, so he pulled *his* .38 and blasted away at the police car as it's zooming away on St. Claude.

"The kid driving the police car *freaked*, as the bullets started hitting the back of the car, shattering the rear window, so he just bailed out and escaped. The police car, still moving at a pretty good clip, finally crashed to a stop; but didn't do much real damage to anything. It was shot full of holes and had its rear and side windows blasted out.

"Of course, the old deputies concocted a glorious

blood-and-guts war story, both deputies became self-proclaimed 'heroes' of this epic gun battle. But the people out there that day saw the whole thing, they knew exactly what had *really* happened, and they had even *less* respect for the deputies than before.

"By the way...*I* was that kid in the car that day..." (Deputy Sheriff)

"The first faults are theirs that commit them, the second, theirs that permit them."

(Anonymous)

THOSE DOGS!

"It was late at night. I was on patrol with my partner, Johnny, out in the Seventh District. They'd sent us on a 21, unknown trouble, on Haynes Boulevard. I forget the address. Anyway, we were having a tough time *finding* the address that night, so we were out there driving around, looking for it. We finally spotted some guy in a little barn-type building shining his flashlight at us, trying to get our attention. We went over there to see what he wanted.

"We had to hop a fence and walk across a large field to get to the man. The guy was behind another fence, in a big yard. The fence had a large 'Beware of Dogs' sign attached to it. The guy had a number of dogs in the yard with him. But, they didn't look particularly dangerous. Johnny asked him, "Hey, Mister, did you call the police?"

"The man said, "Yeah." He had called us, and it was about the dogs killing his chickens. As he talked, the man turned on his flashlight. We spotted the remains of close to thirty chickens out there...torn apart. Not eaten, just killed.

"Johnny and I looked at each other. Johnny said to the man, "Well, Mister, why don't you just tie up your dogs if they're killing your chickens?"

"The man said, "Whoa, I didn't call you guys about these dogs. I want you to take care of *those* dogs!" he said, as he pointed *behind* us.

"We *slowly* turned... In the flashlight beam we saw a Chow, two German Shepards, and various other dogs gazing at us from the darkness. *Big* dogs. Quiet as ghosts..., but their eyes *glowing* in the flashlight's beam. About eight of them.

"Johnny and I were carrying six shot .357 Magnum revolvers loaded with .38 Special ammunition... We had twelve shots between the two of us. I whispered to Johnny, *"We're not gonna win a shootout with those dogs, Johnny. Let's get out of here."* Johnny nodded silently.

"We eased ourselves over to the fence and got over it pronto, and skulked back to our unit and got into it, without incident. We had our Dispatcher call the SPCA to let *them* handle it. Of course, they weren't open for business at that hour, but we found something at the other end of the District, to keep us occupied.

"The next day I went out and bought myself a Beretta M-92 sixteen-shot pistol, and loaded it with the hottest 9mm ammo I could find." (Police Officer)

"One man with courage makes a majority..."
(Andrew Jackson)

THE REAL POLICE

"A while back, Orleans Levee Board Police were detailed to the intersection of Downman Road at Haynes Boulevard for traffic control. We stopped traffic so people could get onto or away from Lakefront Airport. The roadway has been reconfigured now, so the problem has been eliminated. But, back then, we had the detail twice a day. One officer in the morning and two officers were detailed for the heavy afternoon traffic.

"There was a fender bender accident at the intersection, with some substantial property damage to the vehicles involved. I approached the drivers and asked them if they wanted a police report. (We're commissioned officers of the State of Louisiana and have the authority.) But one driver eyeballed my uniform and sneeringly popped off to me, "No, go away. We want *the real police* to handle our accident," meaning the New Orleans Police Department.

"I thought, "*Okay, no problem, less work for me to do.*" It was just after five P.M. or so. I concluded the detail about five-thirty P.M., and took off in my patrol car and resumed regular patrol, and started taking calls for service.

"I passed them again a few hours later. The drivers were still waiting for *the real police* to come handle their accident. They yelled for me to stop, but I ignored them...I already had a call I was responding to. They could have had their accident paperwork handled quickly and competently, but they wanted to fuck with me. So I fucked 'em right back. (Police Officer)

"Police work isn't just a job... it's an adventure!"

The Real Police

(Common saying)

JURISDICTION

"I was working the desk at Troop B. Some man called in and told me he was going to commit suicide. He just wanted us to know about it. He said that he was calling from New Orleans.

"I asked my Sergeant for advice on how to handle the guy. I gave the Sergeant the information I'd obtained, and added that he was calling from New Orleans. My Sergeant told me, "New Orleans? We don't have jurisdiction in New Orleans. Tell him to call the New Orleans Police." (Louisiana State Trooper)

(In late 1995, Louisiana State Troopers were allowed full access to Orleans Parish year round, instead of just during the Mardi Gras season. They had been withdrawn back in the 30s because of a personl issue between the Governor of Louisiana and politicians in New Orleans).

CITIZENS OF THE LAKEFRONT

"I was working overtime on a hot Sunday afternoon. In those days, the off-duty platoon was routinely ordered in for mandatory overtime on Sunday. Seemed like half of New Orleans trooped out to the Lakefront on weekends, and Sunday was particularly bad.

"Imagine a Mardi Gras parade about seven miles long, proceeding one way in an endless loop. Traffic was routed east on Lakeshore Drive. But, the people would make a big loop anyway and drive back along the lakefront. Thousands of people trying to impress each other, mostly teenagers. Beer flowed freely, along with other stuff. It was a big party.

"As you can imagine, even with the one-way traffic flow, we handled our share of fender benders and other traffic problems. Pedestrian traffic was allowed to use the west-bound lanes, so they were filled with bicyclists, joggers, speed-walkers, roller-skaters, skate-boarders, and just plain people. People backing out into each other and causing accidents wasn't unusual.

"We also had to enforce traffic laws, so we wrote moving citations. This time, I'd stopped a young lady, who was driving a snazzy little convertible, for some minor traffic infraction. I was out there all by my lonesome, running her name through M.O.T.I.O.N. for wants and warrants, when I realized that a very large group had appeared around me. Almost all of them teenage boys and young men. They were getting ugly. Usually nothing happened, but, when it did, it just exploded into a mess.

"The angry scowls and muttering didn't upset me as much as the sheer *number* of irritated people around me...several dozen bored and overheated souls guzzling beer and daiquiris, trying to impress each other and their bikini-clad teenyboppers chicks. Group psychology is a funny thing. I realized that one wrong word or move from me could spark the mob into a rage, with me as the focal point of that rage. Well, I'd get my ass kicked... or worse.

"All our other police units were busy. Anyway, with a crowd this size, I would have been stomped flat *long* before any help could arrive. I am renowned for my craziness, so I did something crazy... I looked around, gauged the increasingly hostile mob, and improvised.

"I started talking, "Citizens! I give it to you! This young lady broke the laws of the Lakefront! YOUR laws!"

"I paused, bringing my hands up and addressing the group as I'd seen in all the Roman movies I enjoyed. All I needed was a goddamned toga.

"I went on, "Citizens, what is *your* will? Will she taste death?", I pointed my thumb down, "or embrace life?" I gestured with my thumb up, energetically.

Sorry, Caesar, my apologies, but it was the first thing that came to mind.

"Citizens of the Lakefront, I put her fate in your hands!"

"I could see the hostile faces giving one another incredulous looks, then I saw grins. Laughter broke out. Then cheers!

"Hands, thumbs raised, more cheering, yells, loud laughter. The mob wanted her to live!

"I raised my hands for silence. The crowd, no longer a hostile mob, had settled down and now watched with grinning attention and approval. *They* were part of the action. *They* mattered.

"By your will, good Citizens, I restore her freedom and her life!"

"I turned to the young woman, winked at her, and handed to her her driver's license and registration. "Take these, young lady, go forth, and sin no more!"

"The young lady accepted her documents graciously, smiling and red-faced, got into her little car, and drove away quietly.

"There was wild cheering! The crowd began to dissipate, the entertainment was over, for the time being. They had become part of an epic event. And *I* wasn't going to get killed after all!

"Shaking the hands of grinning former mob members, I strode majestically back to my police unit, got in, cranked it up, and resumed patrol, though I had a hard time keeping a smile off my face." (Police Officer)

"Am I not destroying my enemies when I make friends of them?"
(Abraham Lincoln)

THE CHICKEN CHOKER

"One Sunday morning, a female jogger called in on her cellular phone. She claimed a black man was masturbating in a station wagon out on Lakeshore Drive. She gave us the location and a description of the station wagon. We rolled over there. We spotted the guy and descended upon him.

"He *was* masturbating, as a matter of fact. Very enthusiastically. He was sitting in his station wagon watching passing joggers, choking his chicken like there was no tomorrow. Sick bastard didn't even see us as we rolled up. When we scooped him up and arrested him, he started crying and protesting, telling us we just *couldn't* take him to jail. He had to pick up his mother and sister from church in a little while..." (Police Officer)

"You think I'm paranoid? I know a guy in Narcotics who's so fucked up, he holds a gun on his own reflection in the mirror when he shaves... Now that is fuckin' paranoid, pal."

(Detective)

CAB CRUNCH

"We had one of our deputies we called 'Popeye' rolling on a Code 2, just lights but no siren, except at intersections. A drunk idiot came stumbling out of one of the barrooms on Paris Road, believing that the passing police car, with the overheads flashing, was the cab he'd just called for. So the clown ran out there into the street to catch his cab.

"WHAM!

"The drunk got knocked about forty feet, but incredibly, he wasn't badly injured, just bruised and scared shitless. The *real* casualty was 'Popeye'... When he hit the drunk, he nearly had a heart attack.

Poor 'Popeye'...he was just barreling along, *en route* to his call, and never saw the human meteorite until it struck him. He freaked, started trembling. He got so shook up he blew his groceries right there on the side of Paris Road. Poor old 'Popeye'. His eyes were big as coffee cups..." (Deputy Sheriff)

LAPALCO Boulevard on the West Bank isn't named after an individual; it's an acronym for the Louisiana Power and Light Company.

SIGNAL 24

"I was working in Communications when this hysterical woman called in. She was screaming and crying on the phone. I had a hard time trying to get her calmed down so I could help her. I finally got her calmed down, and got her problem sorted out.

"The caller, an old lady, had been sitting quietly on her glassed-in porch, enjoying her afternoon tea when a bird came zooming along and smacked into the glass. It startled the old lady. When she went over to see what had happened, she saw the bird flopping around in her yard. She was convinced the bird was injured. She wanted a deputy to come over, get it, and take it to a vet for emergency medical treatment for its 'broken pecker'...

"So, with a little smile, I put it out. "Headquarters to one-fifteen."

"One-fifteen, go ahead, Headquarters," replied the bored deputy.

"Signal 24 at (address deleted), a subject down in the back yard with a *broken pecker*."

As you can imagine, I got a slew of laughing 10-9s from other deputies and curious telephone calls from people at home listening to their police scanners." (Deputy Sheriff)

"Damn those who said our good things before us."
(Aelius Donatus)

BADGE 1544

You might notice materials from P.A.N.O. (Police

Association of New Orleans) with the Star-and-Crescent NOPD Badge Number 1544. That Badge was worn by Patrolman Peter E. Bergeron, who fell in the line of duty in 1969. He was the first member of P.A.N.O. to die serving the citizens of New Orleans. His badge number is retained to honor him and his sacrifice.

One veteran Officer, who asked to remain anonymous, added, "And it's a reminder of the sacrifice that any one of us might be called upon to make." The Officer added, "Rest easy, Pete. We didn't forget you, Brother. We never will." (Author)

(Author's Note: As I finish writing this book in early 1996, there have been three metro area policemen killed in the line of duty in one terrible week, all from different departments. One of them was a personal friend of mine).

BONES

"I was giving a homicide investigation lecture to a bunch of trainees. I was giving them a few facts. One of the points I made was that the normal human body contained 209 bones, depending upon which reference book you pick up. That was my point..., that even experts disagree.

"One of the female trainees leaned over to the guy sitting next to her, and whispered something in his ear. His face got red, he glanced at me, and he put his head down.

"This disturbed my lecture. I am a real prick with classroom protocol. So, I asked the female trainee to stand up and tell the entire class what she had told the young man, perhaps it would be something we could *all* enjoy.

"She didn't hesitate an instant. She got right up there and told us, "I told him that there was only *one* bone in my body that interests me, *and its in his pants!"*

"The poor guy turned redder than ever, but all the rest of us, myself included, just *roared!"* (Author's experience)

The United States Secret Service was formed in 1865.

FINE ASS

"I used to have a black woman in my platoon. She was a character, and became my new partner.

"We got a call about a dead body found floating in Lake Pontchartrain, by the west wall of Lakefront Airport. She got all excited. She wanted to go see the dead body. She had never seen a *real* dead body before, except in a funeral home, so we rolled over there.

"This guy had been floating in Lake Pontchartrain for something like *three weeks*. He was pretty ripe, you could smell him over a hundred yards away.

"My new partner got all excited. She wanted to go over and see him close up. I told her to go ahead, to knock her lights out. She exploded out of the police car and went right up to the body and really checked him out. She amused me.

"We had to wait for the guys from the Coroner's Office to come get him, so I walked around and observed my partner eagerly checking out the dead man. I was wondering how she was dealing with the sight and smell of the dead man, because he was really a sight, if you know what I mean.

"Finally, the Coroner's people got there. We got the paperwork completed. Two Parish Prison volunteers scooped up the body and put it in a heavy black zipper bag, hoisted him into the black Coroner's Office van, and took him away. You could smell him, though. That area would smell bad for *months...*

"I asked my partner what she had thought of her first dead man call, and d'ya know what that crazy bitch told me?

"Wow, that boy had a *really fine ass!*"

"I was concerned about her mental state. Some people react badly to handling a decomposing body. But, she hit me with *that* comment.

"Right then I knew she was one of *us...* another sicko." (Police Officer)

First execution by gas chamber: Gee John, murderer, on 8 February 1924.

EVERBODY HAS A STORY

"Once upon a time, early in my career, I was a hot dog. An asshole. I knew *everything* and didn't need any advice from anybody. I can't believe I was that dumb once. Anyway, as I indicated, I had a serious attitude problem. I hated bums...street people. Despised 'em. I'd run 'em up the street, roust them at night. I made their lives miserable.

"But there was this old guy that was sort of different from

the others. He was a little special. I'd given him some crap, but he had this little air about him, this innate sense of dignity, and he never seemed to mind it when I came down on him. He seemed to be amused by my antics.

"After a while, we developed a sort of truce. Later on, I used to talk with him...a lot. He was actually quite an interesting man. Would you believe that the old boy had once been a lawyer? True... I checked into his story and he was actually a respected attorney at one time. But something went wrong in his life, and he started hitting the bottle. Ultimately, he lost everything...his career, his family, his 'friends,' his home, and his self-respect. He missed *that* most of all...

"He taught me that even street people are human beings, and they have feelings, too. Before, I'd assumed they were just part of the landscape. That's how messed up I was when I was twenty-two years old!

"Later on, he kind of took me under his wing. He taught me a lot of things. We developed a good relationship, we did. That old man was sharp as a tack when he wasn't scrambled on the booze. He taught me the valuable lesson that *everybody* has a story. I just had to learn how to listen to them.

"His advice was invaluable to me later, when I became a detective. One evening he wasn't out there. He'd been killed crossing Decatur Street the night before; and, when I found out, I cried like a fuckin' baby." (Detective)

> *"Public's got a right to know? Let me tell you something, Mister: You stick that microphone in my face one more time, and the public is gonna see me shove it right up your ass."*

(Author)

NO PITY

"One day this big, tough motorcycle cop got himself clobbered out on St. Bernard Highway, right by the Chalmette Monument. His own fault... He pulled a little stunt to show me how cool he was, and he busted his ass. One minute, he was cruising along on his big Harley, and seconds later, he's rolling and bouncing along the highway, losing bits of skin and uniform as he slid along.

"I got there fast and looked him over. He was a *mess*. The carefully tailored skin-tight pants, the long, shiny black boots, the tailored uniform shirt and shiny skid-lid were all history. The big Harley-Davidson was badly wrecked, too. It was in pieces all over the road.

"The deputy...call him 'Louie,' was lying there moaning and groaning. I walked up to him. I asked him the proverbial stupid question, because I can plainly see that he was *not* okay, but I went along with convention, "Hey, Louie, buddy, are you okay?"

"Louie turned his head and looked up at me, towering above him. He looked like he was in considerable pain. I kneeled down next to him and helped him remove his ruined biker's helmet.

"Jimmy, how's my bike?" he asked.

"I knew from experience that all *real* bike cops worry about their bikes first and everything else takes a distant second.

"How's my bike?" he asked again.

"I gave it to him straight... I looked him right in the eye. I said, "Well, sorry, buddy, your bike looks like a total fucking write-off. It's scattered from the Parish line to Yscloskey."

"I stood up and looked him over. I coldly kicked his helmet away. "And I think *you're* gonna die, too. Can I have your stereo?" my feeble attempt at humor. 'Louie' was *not* amused, but there wasn't a lot he could do about it at the moment.

"Soon, civilians were making their way toward us, concern on their faces. 'Louie' was lying there, blood, uniform ripped all to shit and most of it missing...

"He'd *definitely* had better days.

"We could hear sirens approaching from the responding ambulances and other police units. Hell, it could have been a lot worse...*I* could have been lying there, or worse, *I* could get stuck doing the mountain of paperwork. Oh well...

"Motioning to me urgently, 'Louie' wanted to tell me something. I went over to him and kneeled down. 'Louie' was trying desperately to cover himself as the civilians approached.

"I bent over him as he whispered in my ear, "Jimmy..., Jimmy..., please don't let them see my peepee!"

"I busted out laughing and stood up, relieved. I knew how tough he was, and I knew if he was worried about strangers looking at his dick, he was going to be okay." (Deputy Sheriff)

The first Federal law enforcement agencies in-cluded the Revenue Cutter Service, Postal Agencies, and Treasury Enforcement.

SO YOUNG

"I was leaning over the victim, a young black male, careful not to get my coat into the wet stuff on the asphalt. The congealing mess...a mixture of blood, grayish brain matter, flecks of white bone, and unrecognizable liquid tissue, was oozing out of the evacuated cranium of the victim. I peered at the devastating crater in the forehead...a single entry wound, very close or contact range. Hard to tell with the massive damage. Blood and tissue loss was extensive. The skull had literally exploded apart when the shotgun's muzzle was pressed against his forehead and fired.

"A little disagreement over a drug transaction had turned lethal. Two dozen people had seen the killing, but only one, a tough old black woman, was willing to talk to the police. The killer had been 'burned' in a dope deal with the victim, so he returned with a friend and a shotgun. There was a little argument, and the arrogant dealer, my victim, had told the man with the shotgun to go 'fuck himself.'

"I was looking at his response. Through the blood and oozing tissue, I could make out stippling and powder burns on the distorted ruin of the forehead, along with what appeared to be an imprint of the shotgun's muzzle. The expanding hot gasses from the muzzle blast had exploded into the victim's skull and displaced his eyes. They had blown out and lay grotesquely across his bloody cheeks.

"The back of his head had ruptured. Bits of bone and splattered tissue were visible over twenty feet away, even in the poor light. The victim's mouth was open. He appeared to be saying, "Oh?" as he lay there, strangely relaxed, flies already buzzing in his gore.

"I stood up and shook my head. Another acolyte for Thanatos. "How old did she say he was?", I asked my partner, who glanced down at his notebook.

"He glanced at me, frowned, and replied, "Here it is... He was thirteen." (Author's experience)

"The belief in a supernatural source of evil is not necessary; men alone are quite capable of every wickedness."
(Joseph Conrad)

THE DOTTED LINE

"I was attending this guy's autopsy. Before they sliced him open, I checked out his tattoos... He was pretty well covered. He had tattoos all over his chest, back, and down his arms and legs. He even had a fly tattooed on the head of his dick. *That* must have felt good.

"This guy, a murder victim, had some really interesting slogans and cartoons on him. He was like a human comic book. Some of the tattoos were really funny, too. Around his neck was a series of dashes, and the legend "Cut on dotted line."

"No shit! I started smiling when I noticed it. He had the same design running down his chest, from throat to navel, the dashes, and "Cut on dotted line." He'd made it so *easy* for the mid-line incision.

"I just shook my head. What a considerate guy. I couldn't stop grinning." (Detective)

"Truth sits upon the lips of dying men."
(Matthew Arnold)

TO DEATH?

"We were at the Orleans Parish Coroner's Office to see the post mortem (autopsy) on a homicide victim. I was breaking in a new partner, a woman. A real debutante. She was fucking *nuts.* Anyway, we passed this guy on one of the cutting tables. He was *very* well equipped. You couldn't help noticing this guy's pecker, he was enormous. A human tripod.

"My partner spotted him, of course, and really zeroed in on the dead guy's pride and joy. She looked at it wistfully, then moved over to me. She glanced at the other people, then whispered up in my ear, "I don't know what killed that guy, Prine, but if I had run into him yesterday *I* might have...I'd have fucked that big boy to *death*." (Author's experience)

"All the things I really like to do are either immoral, illegal, or fattening."
(Alexander Woollcott)

ENEMA

"We had this Code 3 call. We really move when we get a Signal 24, which is an ambulance request. My partner was an old pro, he knew the ropes, but I was still pretty new. Anyway, we got to the scene of this big emergency... We're lugging oxygen tanks, an EKG machine and defibrillator, the drug box, a crash kit, the whole nine yards. Supposed to be a bad heart attack. We'd been dispatched on a heart attack. When we get there, it's an *enema!*

"This old woman hasn't crapped in a week, so she thinks she needs an emergency enema. She lied to the Sheriff's Office dispatcher about the heart attack because she wanted faster service. She was one of our 'frequent fliers', a habitual bullshit caller, but we always responded like it was legitimate call until we knew better.

"My partner, plainly disgusted, said to her, "Lady, the only way you'll get an enema right now is if my boot squirts water when I kick you up your ass." (Deputy Sheriff)

Police Dogs were first used by an American police department in 1906.

KEEP AN EYE ON THIS!

"On my first murder scene, I discovered how demented homicide detectives *really* are. This veteran homicide detective handling the scene was in Homicide when Moses was in third grade...he was legendary. Anyway, this was my first murder scene. I guess I looked a little 'raw.' The detective noticed me, of course, and played his little joke.

"This was a shooting. The detective picked something up off the floor, came over to me, and carefully put it in my hand. I was *so* eager to please. He told me, "Here, son, keep an eye on this, I might need it later. Don't let anyone else have it. And...thanks."

"He seemed so sincere and fatherly. I felt so privileged to be helping such a great man. After he had wandered off to another part of the scene, I finally remembered the object in my hand, what he had placed there. I looked down at it, the thing he had told me to keep an eye on, and I couldn't recognize it. Then realization hit me...it was a fucking eye...an *eyeball!* And the asshole didn't even crack a smile." (Police Officer)

"Homicide dicks are strange motherfuckers. If you're alive and healthy, they don't give a shit about you. But wind up dead someplace and those same guys treat you like you were something special..."

(Police Officer)

JUST LIKE THE ARMY

"You know, working for this department is just like being in the Army. We both run around all night in funny clothes, carrying guns. We have to do stupid things for ignorant people. People try to kill us, and we can't kill them back. If we fuck up a little, we get in trouble with the brass. If we fuck up big time, we get crippled or killed. At least we get a medal and a pretty funeral if we get killed..., just like in the Army. And, if we pull a really bone-headed, super stupid stunt, and don't get cripped or killed, we get kicked out or promoted...just like the Army." (Police Officer)

The U.S. Customs Service was formed in 1927.

NATURAL CAUSES

"What did this guy die of?" asked one detective.

The other replied, "Natural causes."

"The first detective frowned, checked his clipboard, and said, "No, this says he died of multiple gunshot wounds."

"The second detective, a real character, replied, "Hey, dummy, in the Project, multiple gunshot wounds *are* natural causes." (*Overheard at the Orleans Parish Morgue*)

Louisiana Revised Statute 33:1625 requires the Orleans Parish Coroner to make an autopsy 'in all cases of violent death, even though no criminal responsibility might be involved.' The Coroner has other duties as well, including issuing Orders for Protective Custody, OPCs, for individuals suffering from psychiatric problems.

NIGHT DIVE

"I was at home goofing off when the phone rang. It was Headquarters. Some guy had drowned in Lake Pontchartrain, and I was ordered in to make the body recovery.

"I got to HQ fast and started breaking out the underwater search and rescue equipment and the SCUBA gear. Police Dive Team members started showing up: Lt. Ray Hollard, Sgt. Eric Barton, Patrolman Jimmy Schnepf, and myself. Sgt. Barton was going to coordinate the operation from shore.

"We assembled our gear and loaded it into police cars, then drove to the scene of the alleged drowning. It was in the 5000 block of Lakeshore Drive, between Franklin Avenue and the Seabrook Bridge, close to Shelter Number Four.

"A young black man had reportedly been swimming around in Lake Pontchartrain's filthy green waters, and witnesses told us that he had disappeared under the surface at approximately seven-thirty P.M. He never came back up. The scene was well controlled when we arrived. There were a few NOPD and EMS units parked nearby, and, of course, Orleans Levee District Police cars.

"Levee District Officers were controlling access to the scene, keeping unauthorized persons away. We started setting up the gear and Lt. Hollard and Sgt. Barton surveyed the area. Schnepf and I suited up fast, experts at this sort of operation. We'd certainly done it enough times.

"I wore my orange cotton jumpsuit, open-water SCUBA gear including an aluminum 80-cubic foot air tank, a white plastic bicyclist's helmet, a dive mask, fins, and carried three knives and a small SONAR unit. The helmet was to protect my head in the inky blackness of Lake Pontchartrain, littered with chunks of concrete, shards of glass, rusting parts from vehicles and household appliances, and other junk the local citizenry decided to consign to the Lake's depths.

"The knives, razor sharp, were to cut my way out of the assorted lengths of monofilament fishing line, crab-trap line, rope, electrical wire, and other ingenious traps I'd be certain to swim into during the search.

"We knew better than to use underwater lights; the suspended particles in the lake's turbid depths made them impractical. My battered, stainless steel Rolex Submariner diver's watch, which I'd bought in Vietnam, was securely snapped to my left wrist. The Rolex and I were veterans of body recovery dives, cave dives, parachute jumps, and years of police and military assignments. It was a trusted friend and sort of a good-luck charm.

"Suited up, I eased my way down the steps of the concrete seawall, careful not to slip on the green slime coating the last few steps. Barnacles, sharp as scalpel-blades, crusted the steps. A bad fall on them meant a trip to the Hospital.

"It was early September, still quite warm, and Lake Pontchartrain was calm. Peaceful. A light breeze made gentle waves on the oily surface. I shook my head as I wrinkled my nose...Lake Pontchartrain smelled like a gigantic cesspool.

"Not long before, two "A" teams of Army Special Forces troopers, 'Green Berets,' had been in town for one reason or other, and had decided to use the Lake for helocast training. This required them to jump out of helicopters into the Lake, from various heights and speeds. One of the Special Forces medical sergeants had checked samples of Lake Pontchartrain's water and absolutely forbid the troopers' using the Lake. "It'd be like brushing your teeth with a turd!" he told me. It meant a lot to me, a police diver, to be diving in polluted water too filthy for Green Berets to use.

"A sickly yellow moon hung high in the clear summer night, casting a gloomy light over the scene. Actually, it was a beautiful evening. Regular people were driving along Lakeshore Drive just a few feet behind us, probably admiring the fine evening and viewing the flashing police strobes and police cars with idle curiosity. I was preparing to launch myself into the warm, dark, bacteria-laden waters of Lake Pontchartrain and grope around for a dead man. I looked over at Schnepf and grinned.

"Schnepf grinned back. Good old Schnepf...cool, professional, and an expert diver. Schnepf was a former commercial diver and a veteran of several years' service in the Fourth District, across the river. He made an excellent partner, and was just the kind of man you wanted with you on something like this.

"Other cops made the scene, too. I glanced up and spotted Major Petersen, just retired from the NOPD and one of the few Levee District cops I truly admired and respected without qualification. Lt. Sue Eagan, an eager sport diver and the Levee District's Training Officer, made her way gingerly down the concrete steps and checked our SCUBA gear with her flashlight. She seemed anxious. By this time, Hollard and Barton, both highly experienced in body recoveries in this area, had made up a plan on how to conduct the search. Hollard started suiting up. In a minute or so, he was ready and Lt. Eagan helped him down the treacherous sea wall. We were ready.

"We jumped out carefully, avoiding the concrete sea wall and its sheath of barnacles, our Scubapro buoyancy compensators partially inflated to keep us floating on the surface. As we hit the water, schools of mullet darted away, startled by our abrupt appearance.

"There was a slight current, and we knew the water below us was only ten or twelve feet deep. The three of us bunched together and Hollard informed Schnepf and I of the plan. It was a good one, but then Hollard and Barton were seasoned professionals, and we expected no less. We all agreed on the final details, nodded our assent, then prepared to submerge.

"I made certain my gear was snug but not tight, and nothing was missing. My knives were in easy reach. My dive tank's air pressure gauge indicated just over three thousand pounds pressure, so I had plenty of breathing gas. My helmet was secure, and my mask was sealed perfectly. I clenched the mouthpiece of my air regulator, took a few experimental breaths to be certain it was performing satisfactorily, and started slowly venting air from my buoyancy compensator. I started sinking. To the spectators atop the sea wall, our three heads slowly disappeared into the dark depths.

"The images: my helmet, my left hand holding the B.C. hose overhead, the tranquil night, our singular task, and the expectation of the waiting crowd...I had a weird thought as I sank beneath the gentle waves... *"Ave, Caesar, morituri te salutamus!"*... the gladiators' traditional salutation to a Roman emperor as they prepared for combat in the arena.

"We sank slowly onto the silty, garbage, and trash-laden floor of Lake Pontchartrain, *our* arena this evening, and we hooked up and began the first search pattern. There was no cheering crowd to appreciate our victory, or our death if something unfortunate happened...we would act out our little drama beyond the eyes of the crowd above. And one man was already dead.

"People ask me, "What do you think about when you're swimming around in the dark, looking for a dead person?" I usually change the subject quickly, or blow them off in the standard gruff policeman's manner. But I'll tell you what I *really* think about...nothing in particular, Whatever seems appropriate. I don't have visions of giant, hungry sharks or the odd killer octopus, what the public seems to think we worry about. No, I just keep my eyes closed and swim. You can't *see* anything, and in Lake Pontchartrain, you wouldn't *want* to see it anyway.

"I'd learned to keep my eyes closed for a simple psychological reason...the way our brains are wired. I'd discovered that if you swim around in the darkness, unable to see anything, but with your eyes open, your mind will start *manufacturing* images for you to 'see', and they are never good. But if you keep your eyes closed, you avoid all that nonsense. Anyway, it worked for me well enough.

"I don't worry about the dead person coming up and grabbing me, or any of that nonsense, although one of our divers, Sgt. Gavin Pagart, once *did* make the fastest search and recovery I'd ever heard of. He jumped off the breakwater near the Seabrook Bridge and actually *landed* in the *arms* of a drowned person. He launched out of the Lake like a Polaris missile!

"I was not at all curious about the man we were searching for. I hoped he'd accomplished most of the things he had set out to do, and had enjoyed a happy and productive life. I hoped he had someone to miss him, but also hoped they wouldn't be devastated by his loss. I wondered if I'd get to meet him on the 'other side', and what kind of person he'd been. No, I didn't think about the man at all. He was, as the Air Traffic Controllers say, "no longer a factor"... he'd lived his life but now it was over.

"We swam along the bottom, totally blind. Schnepf was on my left, and Hollard was on *his* left. My SONAR unit wasn't much good, I couldn't even read its display in the murky water. It was like diving in ink. We were maintaining physical contact as we swam along...the only practical way to stay in touch in those conditions. We swam and swam, changing course as needed to maintain the pattern, counting fin kick cycles and times to maintain the search pattern. Our hands groped in the darkness...they became our antennae. We slid them across various textures in the blackness...sharp, slimy, hard, soft. I'd seen the used sanitary napkins, the syringes and medical waste fished out of the water we were swimming through now.

"As I sliced my fingers repeatedly, I remembered the Jefferson Parish Sheriff's Office LASER ("Land, Air, Sea, Emergency Rescue") diver who had cut up his hands on a dive, too, and something nasty had entered his body...the infection grew out of control, and eventually, the doctors had to amputate most of his hand to save his life.

"Once, *something* big grabbed Skip Revolta on a night dive in the Lake. It grabbed him and shook him savagely, then let go. Luckily for Skip, it had grabbed onto his diving tank instead of his head. If left impressive tooth marks in the tough aluminum diving tank, but Skip was uninjured. We never did find out what it was.

"After a while, my legs started to feel the strain from the constant swimming. My mouth and throat were completely dried out from breathing the dry, filtered compressed air from the SCUBA tank..., a condition we call 'cotton mouth.'

"In Florida springs and cave systems, the water used to be pure and clear, and all you needed to do to get a refreshing drink was to remove your regulator and swallow a few mouthfuls of cold, clear spring water. I've even carried plastic squeeze containers of Gatorade and fruit juices to keep myself hydrated during long dives. I've even eaten oranges underwater, during long decompression stops. Lots of cave divers do it.

"In Lake Pontchartrain, we just suffered through it. In due time, our air ran low and we had to get out of the water to change over to fresh air tanks. This was swiftly accomplished. Lt. Eagan was really hustling, and Barton hovered over us like a big black mother hen. We were back in the water in no time. The crowd was bigger than before, and getting restive. I guess they wanted TV-style action and they were apparently overdue for a commercial break...

"We resumed the search and suddenly, I found the drowned victim...I literally swam right into him. The impact almost knocked off my dive mask. My partners *knew* I had him...I broke contact and started making 'hoots' through my regulator to let them know. I grabbed the man's body tightly; I didn't want him to get away from me, and, for the merest instant, I had the impulse to *handcuff* him so he couldn't escape...a policeman's reflex, instantly squelched.

"Hollard and Schnepf surfaced first, to let the shore party know we'd found the victim, and I slowly ascended as well, keeping the dead man's body below the surface so the morbid couldn't see his face. I'd never met the man, but I knew he wouldn't want to be seen in this condition, and I felt fiercely protective of him. Living or dead, he had a right to some dignity. And, he undoubtedly had family members ashore, and I wanted to spare them as much as possible.

"We swam in with the victim, towing him gently, TV reporters' lights in our eyes making navigation easy and vision impossible. We manhandled him up out of the water onto the seawall, and Barton and the shore party took him away from us. I was exhausted and gulped in the fresh evening air hungrily. It was sweet and wonderful.

"The victim had been about thirty yards out, laying face down on the bottom in about twelve feet of water. It was ten-thirteen P.M., and we had accomplished another successful recovery." (Author's experience)

"The last enemy that shall be destroyed is death."
(Saint Paul)

BOOM BOOM

"We had a Deputy named Bob. He bought an Ithaca Model 37 riot shotgun...a 12-gauge pump gun with rifle sights and a satin nickel finish. A very pretty gun. It had cost Bob two hundred dollars plus tax. He'd bought it from a gun dealer on Paris Road in Chalmette; and, as a matter of fact, I was with him when he bought it. Boy, was Bob proud of his new cannon!

"A week later, we were getting off from the four-to-twelve evening shift. Bob had just gone outside with his new Ithaca, preparing to go home. Most of the other guys were still in the squad room, cutting up and letting off steam.

"Suddenly, there was a loud 'BOOM!' We all looked around at each other. Another 'BOOM!' We all ran outside to see what was going on. We saw Bob hobbling around in the clam shell parking lot.

"He yelled, "I'm okay, I'm okay...I just shot myself..."

We just stared at him, in silent amazement.

"... TWICE!" he continued, as he stumbled around, leaving a respectable blood trail.

"We all burst out laughing hysterically at Bob's misadventure...none of us tried to help him. We couldn't...we were laughing.too hard, and besides, Bob was an excellent medic and he wouldn't come to harm.

Bob was more embarrassed than injured. Of course we instantly named him "Boom Boom"... He really loved *that* nickname, too...

"The next day, Bob sold me his beloved Ithaca for just fifty bucks." (Deputy Sheriff).

The first version of the Star-and-Crescent badge worn by New Orleans Police Officers appeared in 1852. The Superintendent of NOPD traditionally wears a special upside-down version of the badge.

THE GRENADE

"One day I was at home monitoring my police radio...I usually keep it tuned to the primary dispatch channel, so I know what's going on. I was just getting out of the bathtub when they started talking about a store security guard finding a hand grenade and delivering it to our detail officer working the shopping mall. Apparently, it was a real grenade, because they called the Jefferson Parish Sheriff's Office Bomb Squad for assistance.

"Headquarters informed the detail officer that the JPSO Bomb Squad was tied up with something over on the East Bank, and it would be over an hour until they could get someone out to take care of the hand grenade. The detail officer was sort of nervous...you should have heard his voice on the radio. He'd had no experience with hand grenades or any kind of explosives, and he was begging for someone...*anyone*...to come and get the grenade from him. I smiled.

"*I* was *very* familiar with them, so I telephoned Headquarters and told them that I'd be going right over to help the detail officer with the grenade. I asked Headquarters to have the officer tape the 'spoon' on the grenade down, so, even if the pin was pulled, it wouldn't go off. I got dressed and went over there fast.

"The Day Platoon Sergeant had already arrived, and both he and the detail officer were wrapping the entire grenade with white surgical tape...there must have been thirty yards of tape wrapped around the grenade when I arrived.

"Sometimes, crazy people cram black powder or other material into practice grenades and substitute smoke grenade fuses, with have zero delay detonation, to make 'hand grenades.' But, pull the pin on one of those things and "WHAM!'...instant explosion. Every so often you read about kids playing with lethal toys and getting maimed or killed.

"After removing most of the tape and closely examining the grenade, I told the Sergeant and the detail officer that it looked all right, and that it was probably just a practice grenade...an inert casing used for throwing and familiarization. You can buy them at pawn shops, gun shows, and surplus stores. I told the Sergeant that, if I removed the fuse mechanism, it would be safe, in any event. He told me to go ahead and make it safe.

"Now, we were out on the edge of the parking lot, over a quarter mile from any people or property. If it *was* a live grenade and went off, no one would have been injured, except for *me*. I started to remove the fuse mechanism. Carefully. You never know...

"The Sergeant said, "Hold up, Mister. You get back there a ways with that thing. I don't want your blood and guts all over my unit."

"He was concerned about getting his car *dirty!* He didn't mind if I got myself eviscerated and had my hands blown off, but he didn't want to have his car messed up. I chuckled, and removed the fuse mechanism.

"As I suspected, it was just an inert casing. No danger to anyone. I gave it to the detail officer for a souvenir. The Sergeant canceled the JPSO Bomb Squad. I went home. But, don't ever think for a minute that all cops are on the same wavelength when it comes to priorities." (Police Officer)

The good you do dies with you, but your fuck ups are forever..."

(Police saying)

THE MAN WHO TRIED TO KILL GOD

"One afternoon, I had a confrontation with a man who was trying to kill God. I was working a traffic detail on Ben Weiner (a Tulane University Campus street) and South Claiborne Avenue. Next to the Rosen House. I was there maintaining one-way traffic flow, because of construction in the area.

"This sweaty black dude came along, kinda shuffling. No shirt, no shoes, and sort of dirty looking. He had smears of fresh blood on his arms and chest. He was swinging a big machete that must have been three feet long. He was talking to himself, making swipes with the machete, and he directed his weird red eyes at me.

"As I saw this, I said to myself, *"I'm fucked... Why do the crazy people always come after me?"*

"I got out of the police car and told the man hello. He ignored me, but made an impressive swipe with that big-ass knife.

"I was *very* impressed. I tried to talk to the man, and, meanwhile, I was remembering my Officer Survival training... If he got within twenty feet of me with that thing, swinging it like that, I was going to start shooting.

"I saw an image of the inquest... *"Yessir, I felt myself in imminent danger of being killed or receiving great bodily harm, so I fired a warning magazine into the subject's chest."*

"I got on the radio and requested backup on a Code 3, keeping my radio keyed a few seconds so the other troops could hear the crazy man's mumbling, and to get it all on tape. I was trying to stay calm and keep my pulse rate below two hundred.

"The man suddenly yelled, *"GOD! GOD! I'M HERE TO KILL YOU! COME ON DOWN HERE SO I CAN KILL YOU!"*

"The man was still moving my way, and I was becoming concerned. He spurned my overtures of friendship. I half expected to see a '666' appearing on his forehead, or plumes of green vomit, or hopefully, a rotating head display, but no luck. Not even a lightning bolt. Just a crazy man with a big-ass knife...

"At least there were no civilians around for him to slice up. Just me. On the other hand, passing traffic on South Claiborne was definitely interested in our tableau.

"Lt. Harry Steinkamp rushed up in the electric Supervisor's cart. The day watch commander, Steinkamp dismounted and walked over to me, concern on his face.

"I pointed at the approaching crazy man with the big knife. Steinkamp looked at him, heard the angry threats at God, and his eyes widened.

"I told him, "Hey, Lieutenant, we can make a case. We can charge the guy with Aggravated Assault on a Deity, but I don't remember if that's the in the Municipal Code."

"Steinkamp looked at the crazy man, then, disgusted, he turned to me. "Why do you do this shit to me? I put you out here on a routine traffic detail, and you dig up a guy trying to kill God! Only *you* could do this to ME!" he yelled.

"He was pissed. As usual, all this was *my* fault.

"Steinkamp pointed his beefy finger at me. "The Second District is rolling, so don't let this guy kill anybody until they can drag him off!" he ordered.

"No problem, I just hoped the madman kept his blade to himself. In seconds, we could hear the NOPD units zooming in on a Code 3.

"No response from the guy, or his big knife. He just stood

there, swishing his big knife, and eye-fucking us.

"The blue-and-white NOPD cars came in fast, disgorging patrol cops with strange looks on their faces. One of them asked what the fuck was going on.

"Lt. Steinkamp told them all. He pointed at the man, still ambling around swishing his machete, and threatening God. "That man just threatened to kill God with his machete," Steinkamp told the NOPD cops, "Get him out of here, please."

"The NOPD Officers encircled the would-be God-killer, talked nicely to him, and showed him their shiny Beretta pistols. The crazy man apparently realized he wasn't going to win *this* round. Smiling, he threw down his machete, which clattered on the street as the NOPD guys swarmed him, 'cuffed him, then helped him into one of the units for the drive to Charity's third floor...the psycho ward.

"One of the other NOPD guys walked over, picked up the machete, looked at us, and laughed. He took the machete and drove away, grinning and shaking his head.

"Before Steinkamp left, he pointed that finger at me again, and ordered me to "just do your job, and quit starting trouble!" (Police Officer)

SGT. GILBERT J. MAST, TULANE DEPARTMENT OF PUBLIC SAFETY, WAS KILLED IN THE LINE OF DUTY ON 20 JANUARY, 1996. SGT. MAST WAS THE FIRST TULANE POLICE OFFICER TO GIVE HIS LIFE IN THE PERFORMANCE OF HIS DUTY. HE WAS A REAL POLICEMAN TO THE LAST.

COLD BLOW

One night in the Fifth District, it was so cold, you wouldn't believe it. No calls, no backlog...no *nothing.* The entire District was like a ghost town...*nothing* was moving.

"My partner was knocked out, snoring, and I was just driving around in the unit trying not to freeze to death. It was something like four in the morning.

"I turned left off Caffin Avenue onto Florida Avenue, just cruising slowly with the lights off. So what did I see?

"Out there on Florida Avenue, just west of Egania, there was a woman giving this dude a blowjob...right there on the side of the street!

"In freezing cold weather!

"And they were *outside* the car...the guy was leaning back across the hood, and she was down there giving him an Olympic-class Gold Medal blowjob. She never looked up, but the dude checked me out as I cruised by...he gave me this little shit-eating, kind of semi-apologetic little grin.

"I was *so* amazed... I didn't really believe I'd see this kind of activity out in *this* weather. I thought my imagination was playing tricks. I must have been hallucinating, right? I kept driving for a little while, then went back there. I had to see. I had to *know*. My curiosity was killing me. But they'd gone...or maybe I *did* crack up a little that night. (Police Officer).

"It has to be admitted that we English have sex on the brain, which is a very unsatisfactory place to have it."

(Malcolm Muggeridge)

BEAM ME UP!

"One time, we were bringing a prisoner to Charity Hospital to get him sewed up...his old lady had cut him up a little in a 103-D (domestic fight). Out came this psycho with the Charity security guys and various hospital and medical-types chasing him. The dude was hauling ass, too... He was *really* making time toward us as we drove up the ambulance ramp.

"The guy saw us..., the *police*..., and he literally slid to a halt. It was just like you see in the cartoons! He started yelling at his hand... *"Scotty! Scotty! Beam me up!Klingons all over down here!"*

"He was serious, too. My asshole partner was looking around for the fucking Klingons, and our prisoner was trying not to piss on himself... he was laughing fit to bust a gut.

"I jumped out and subdued the guy, and then the 'cavalry' arrived to take him away. You see some really *strange* shit in that place." (Police Officer)

"It is his reasonable conversation which mostly frightens us in a madman."

(Anatole France)

BOYS' NIGHT OUT

"We were cruising down Paris Road looking for action, looking for *anything*, and my partner *saw* something. He whipped the unit around. We drove back up a way, over a little levee by the hump on Paris Road. My buddy had seen a brief flash of light from back there in the darkness. Know what we discovered? An older woman having fun with her 'boyfriends.' *Lots* boyfriends. She had a few six-packs of beer she'd brought along with her, and she was having group sex with *all* of them...an *entire* Little League baseball team! She was getting them drunk and screwing all of them. That sicko bitch. Luckily for us, it was a quiet night, and nothing else was going on, because we had to get the entire platoon to ferry the kids over to the Courthouse, so we could begin to sort things out and start notifying all the kids' parents to come over and get them. A lot of the little punks had never drunk anything before, and they started getting sick and blowing their groceries everythere. And some of them were crying and raising hell and screaming. What a nightmare. We threw the book at the woman, too. Boy, that was one night I'll *never* forget." (Deputy Sheriff)

Historically, law enforcement is charged with the preservation of public order and the prevention and detection of crimes.

THE FOOT EATER

"One night, I was working Cental Control in the lockup. Sergeant De Noux, in Intake Booking, called us about a prisoner they'd just booked. The guy was acting up badly and was threatening to commit suicide.That meant special precautions had to be taken, so they processed the man and brought him over to us. We were better equipped to monitor him closely.

"He was a white male, about twenty-seven years old and a real funkball. You wouldn't believe how *dirty* the guy was! Anyway, the lieutenant and some deputies got the guy stripped down. They had a really hard time with his shoes and socks... The socks had been on his feet so long they were sort of glued onto his feet.

"After the guy was stripped down and examined, he was placed in a special cell which allowed for easy observation. We had to watch over him *very* closely, because of his suicide threats. As soon as he was in the cell, he started acting crazy, screaming and banging his head on the concrete floor, and against the walls. This upset us, because he could have injured himself and blamed us for 'beating him up.' The lieutenant went in there and talked to the guy; told him to calm down or we'd put him in a straitjacket. The guy calmed down a bit, then he sat on the floor and got quiet.

"A short time later, the lieutenant went over to the observation window. His eyes got wide.

"He yelled, "Jesus Christ! This guy can't be from *this* planet! The motherfucker is eating his feet!"

"Interested, I asked him, "How can somebody eat their own feet, lieutenant?"

"Then I jumped down from the console, went over, and looked in, too. I was curious as hell, I'd never even heard of someone eating their own feet, and I wanted to see for myself how he was doing it...

"The guy was *scraping* strips of meat off his feet...big hunks of meat. He was putting the chunks in his mouth and chewing on them. He was ripping into sores on his arms, opening them up and sucking out blood.

"The lieutenant, a little shook up, said, "I don't *believe* this dude. I've never seen anything like this in my life..."

"I looked in at the guy, who was really going at it...blood was *everywhere*...and told the lieutenant, "Hey, L.T., he's awful scrawny, maybe he's just hungry. Let's feed him something."

"So we made him a couple of mystery meat sandwiches and offered them to the guy. He just *inhaled* them... he didn't bother chewing on them, he just mashed 'em into his mouth and swallowed 'em. He was like some kind of human shark.That was one *strange* motherfucker..." (Deputy Sheriff)

> *"Every normal man must be tempted, at times, to spit on his hands, hoist the black flag, and begin slitting throats."*
>
> *(H.L. Mencken)*

THE FOOTBALL PLAYER

"During this particular incident, I was on foot patrol on McAlister (a Tulane University campus street) walking toward Freret Street. My Sergeant radioed me that there was a 107 (suspicious person) black male coming my way. He provided a clothing description.

"I saw the man and started angling toward him. He saw me and we both locked eyes. Bingo!

"The man started flat-out running toward Freret Street, trying to get off campus.

"I pursued him and started the usual litany... "Police! Stop!" all that good stuff. It had the usual effect...nothing. If anything, the guy just speeded up.

"We were approaching Freret Street rapidly. Tulane students, pedestrians, and other folks were staring goggle-eyed at the action.

"Some crazy Tulane football player saw the chase, and he decided to participate...he *tackled* the guy! He got the man flattened down on the sidewalk and was struggling with him when I ran up.

"The black man was *desperate* to get away. He was really struggling with the football player, wriggling around, kicking, and trying to bite him. Finally, as I called for backup at the location, the guy managed shake off the football player, got up, and he tried to make a run for it.

"But I was right there, and I latched onto him as he rose, and got a good grip on his neck and the back of his shirt and jacket. I was watching his hands, because he looked just like the asshole that had pulled a gun on me the week before.

"RIP! The guy's shirt and jacket ripped off in my hands, so my good hold on him instantly turned to shit. I fell on my ass on the sidewalk. The guy sprang out into Freret Street...right into moving traffic.

"There was a loud *bang!* as some citizen nailed the guy with his car. Everything sort of went into slow motion. I was imagining the civil suit the guy was going to smack *us* with.

"The fleeing subject somersaulted through the air and, would you believe, the son of a gun landed *running?* No kidding, the guy must have been a gymnast, and a damned lucky one.

"The crazy football player was on him in a flash...I don't know how he avoided the passing traffic. They went down in a heap, another fine tackle by the Science building. The fighting started all over again, but with renewed vigor...I guess between the adrenalin and the testosterone, it was too much for them. But now the subject had no shirt or jacket, just rags, and he was slippery as hell.

"Seconds later I had joined them. Understand that by this time my portable radio was gone, lost in the melee, along with various parts of my uniform. I couldn't call for backup.

"The guy was fighting us like a maniac. I couldn't let him get his hands on a gun...not the one in my holster, or the one I'm certain he has. We're punching and kicking, fighting desperately, and *I* was losing. Well, I was the oldest of us, by far, so that was to be expected.

"The black guy was *years* younger than I was. He was in terrific shape, too...they have some excellent weight training in prison. I *knew* he'd been in the system, I just sensed it. He was beating the shit out of the football player *and* me...he was definitely on some good drugs, too.

"That football player was no wimp, and I'm not exactly a

pussy myself. Tired of being on the receiving end of the punishment, I thought, *"Fuck this!"* I pulled my little Smith and Wesson nine millimeter pistol. Punching it into his chest, I told him, "Give it up, motherfucker, calm down and stop fighting, or I'll blow your fuckin' heart out!"

"I wasn't joking, either. I meant *precisely* what I said. I saw the guy's eyes widen as he realized that I was actually going to kill him. It worked.

"He stopped fighting, relaxed, and, trying to catch his breath, said, "You gots me, bro...I gives up." Fair enough. I was out of breath, too, and I'd be sore for days from the beating he'd delivered.

"I was astride this guy with the muzzle of my pistol ground into his chest and suddenly realized that the football player was long gone. Maybe he was late for class or something? I wanted to thank him.

"Trying to catch my breath, I saw my colleagues in the distance, running my way, coming to help. Passers-by looked at my bloody face and torn uniform and the chewed-up looking bad guy. No one wanted a piece of us, except one asshole.

"One of them, probably a goddamned law student, yelled "Police brutality!", but he moved off swiftly. Piss on him.

"After my people got there and took custody of my guy, I was ordered to go to the hospital to get examined. I'd taken some pretty good hits, and there was a large knot on the back of my head where I had struck the concrete. I had patches of skin missing off my hands, elbows, knees, and various other places. My wristwatch was long gone, and no one ever turned it in. It must have vanished to the same place where my nameplate and my ballpoint pens had gone. I even had to buy a new clipboard; mine had been rolled over by a passing car and was a write-off. Someone *did* find my badge, though, and turned it in...probably because it was so scratched up, it was worthless.

"When I got patched up and returned to duty later, I was informed that the guy I'd been chasing and fighting with had been released, with no charges filed. My Lieutenant at the time was an asshole, too, so that was pretty standard. At least I wasn't ordered to apologize to the guy or buy him new clothes or anything. Knowing Tulane, they probably gave him a big chunk of money, to keep him happy.

"Days later, the football player saw me on campus and identified himself as my rescuer. I thanked him for his help, and asked him why he'd left the scene so quickly. *He told me that he didn't want to get full of blood when I shot the guy.*

"The football player was from a little farming community out West. He told me he like to wrestle and play football, but, when people started pulling guns, he wanted out." (Police Officer)

> *"I believe in the brotherhood of all men, but I don't believe in wasting brotherhood on anyone who doesn't want to practice it with me. Brotherhood is a two-way street."*
>
> *(Malcolm X)*

JUNK CAR

"The burned-out car on Judge Perez Drive had been there

for several days. No one bothered checking it. Abandoned or burned vehicles appeared and vanished at random. Regular and routine, you know what I mean?

"The NOPD had sent out a bulletin about a 67-A (stolen) vehicle and added that it had probably been involved in a kidnaping and murder. We got the pertinent information, including the license plate number, and broadcast it to the patrol deputies.

"One of our deputies *found* that stolen car, burned to a crisp, out on Judge Perez Drive. Out in the open, in plain sight. Thousands of people passed by it each day. No one gave it a second glance. Probably just an insurance job or something like that, right?

"The license plate was still legible on the vehicle. In the trunk was the body of the murder victim. He had been bound, placed into the trunk, and shot to death. Sometime later the car had been parked and set afire. We check out abandoned cars a lot more thoroughly now." (Deputy Sheriff)

> *"I hate that term 'routine traffic stop.' Or 'routine patrol'... the only routine thing about police work is that nothing is what it seems to be; you really don't know what's coming at you next."*
>
> *(Author)*

HENRY BONDS

"Yeah, I used to work with Henry Bonds. Henry was a helluva lot of fun to work with...a great guy, very intelligent, always with a smile. He always had loads of jokes to tell, too.

Good ones. He works for Harry Lee now, over in Jefferson.

"Henry is a gifted Accident Investigator, by the way. One night there was a 20-I (accident with injury) out in the Seventh District, on Paris Road. NOPD called us and asked St. Bernard to handle it, because they didn't have any units clear. So we rolled out there to see what we could do.

"A big tractor-trailer had gone off the road and crashed on its side. The driver was trapped in the cab, badly hurt and screaming for help. Trouble was the location, most of the truck was in a little gully, actually part of a canal bed. And the truck was a tanker, loaded with gasoline. The tank had ruptured, and gasoline was gurgling out of the truck and rapidly filling the gully. It was a very dangerous situation... one spark and the driver, the truck, and everyone around gets burned up. Us included.

"We worked in almost complete darkness, because we were afraid to use flashlights. We worked our asses off trying to extricate the driver. Other St. Bernard Deputies were on the roadway directing traffic around the wreck, and keeping civilians away from the hazard area. No highway flares or anything...as I indicated, one spark and we were all toast.

"Down in the gully we were scrambling around, shoving and cursing, trying desperately to save the driver and not get ourselves killed. We were sloshing around in several *inches* of gasoline; the little gully was filling fast. The fumes were very thick, and we were having a hard time dealing with that. I was afraid I was going to pass out and die there in the ditch. We were all scared shitless, let me tell you.

"Then, horror of horrors, some helpful soul discovered the 'Jaws of Life' in the back of the Henry's A.I. (Accident

Investigation) van, DR-25, and decided to get it cranked up.

"When we heard the little two-cycle engine roar to life, Henry and I looked at each other and I knew what each of us was thinking... *"OH SHIT!"*

"One of the other Deputies intervened and shut it off instantly, thank God, and for some reason, we weren't incinerated.

"We managed to save the driver, by the way. He sued us in civil court, but they threw the case against us out. But that lawsuit really made us want to go out and risk our lives for strangers, you know? (Deputy Sheriff)

> *"There is not a more mean, stupid, dastardly, pitiless, selfish, spiteful, envious, ungrateful animal than the public."*
>
> *(William Hazlitt)*

A MIRACLE

"It was early on a Monday morning. I was working in Communications. We had just gone on duty for the day watch. I got a call from a passerby about a car in a canal 'down the road.' I got what information I could from the caller, then dispatched one of the road deputies to check it out. People often dump abandoned vehicles in the canals, so it wasn't an urgent call.

"The deputy went 10-97 (arrived on the scene) a little later. The only visible part of the car was one of its tires protruding from the water. The female deputy saw air bubbles coming from the car. She realized that it might not be just another abandoned car dumped in the water. She radioed in a request for a 'hook' (tow truck), and told us she had a hunch that a person was still in the car. I immediately dispatched a wrecker.

"When the wrecker arrived on the scene, our deputy helped him hook onto the car, and watched him raise it from the canal. There *was* a person in the car... a woman. *And she was still alive!*

"During the subsequent investigation, the woman revealed that she had gotten off from work Friday evening and went out partying. She had had a few drinks and started home. One the way home, she lost control of her car and ran off the road into the canal. She spent the *entire weekend* underwater in her car! You and I know that no automobile holds that much air." (Deputy Sheriff)

> *"A miracle may be accurately defined: a transgression of a law of nature by a particular volition of the Deity, or by the interposition of some invisible agent."*
>
> *(David Hume)*

THE ULTIMATE COUCH POTATO

"We were dispatched on a Signal 24; asked to assist some EMTs with a patient. This pissed us off, because it was beneath our dignity (laugh). We were *cops*, not medics, and usually the EMTs just wanted people with strong backs to help them lift some fat lady or something. Instead of hiring enough people to get their job done, they called us...we always showed up and didn't cost them anything....

"But this call was *different.* Their patient was...well, he was *fused* into a sofa. This old guy lived with his brother, who was a 103-M (mental case). The guy literally lived on a diet of beer, peanuts, potato chips and other shit his brother would dole out to him. He hadn't been off the sofa in *years*, and had literally melted into it...he'd become *part* of it.

"His legs had withered and rotted away, and from the waist down, there was just a dark, wet, stinking mess. Fecal material, urine, body fluids...it all just kinda *oozed* out of the guy, onto the floor. Over the years, all that nasty stuff had eaten a hole in the wooden floor, and all that nasty filth just kinda dripped down through it, The room was tiny, way up in the attic of an old house, and the only access was a narrow stairway. No air conditioning, of course, and it must have been well over a hundred degrees up there. Roaches ran around everywhere...

"The stench was overpowering. I've seen some pretty raunchy shit, over in Vietnam, and over here on the street, but this scene was totally beyond my experience. I was gagging, just being in there with the guy...my partner couldn't even make it up the stairs...it was just too much for him.

"The EMTs didn't look too happy with the situation, either, and they didn't know how to get the guy off the sofa without breaking him in two and killing him. The sofa was too big to get down the tiny stairs; it had been installed using an outside stairwell that had been torn down years before.

"We really didn't know what to do with the guy. As a matter of fact, *he* didn't want to go anywhere, anyway...he was content where he was. He told us that he felt fine, and that he wished we'd just go away and stop bothering him. His psycho brother kept dancing around in the roaches, asking us if we wanted something to eat or drink...he was *beyond* the smell, a total Loony Tunes wacko, and I wanted to *kill* that motherfucker. Finally, I got on the radio and got some assistance, and the poor assholes that made the scene wanted to kill *me* for getting them involved... (Police Officer)

"Schizophrenic behavior is a special strategy that a person invents in order to live in an unlivable situation."

(R. D. Laing)

THE CAR KILLER

"We had this guy named Arnold. Big guy, a former athlete. He had been a deputy for over a year, assigned to the Emergency Medical Service section in Special Operations. He didn't carry a sidearm...he didn't like guns. But one day, the Sheriff saw him without the required sidearm, chewed him out, and ordered him to carry one, or turn in his badge.

"Guns weren't issued by the Sheriff's Office, so that meant that Arnold had to buy or borrow one. Now, understand that Arnold was a convictee felon, and he was forbidden by law to have a firearm, but he didn't want to lose his job, either.

"So, Arnold decided to buy his own gun and he wanted a revolver. He wanted to get the smallest, cheapest thing he could get away with, and he told us he was going to get one of the little two-inch 'belly guns' like a Chief's Special from Smith & Wesson or one of Colt's 'Detective Specials,' which were tiny little .38 Special revolvers. He wanted something small and light...something inconspicuous, something no one would notice.

"So the big dummy came in with a Smith & Wesson Model 27...a huge, heavy-framed .357 Magnum. His was nickel plated, and had the target setup... the fancy trigger and sight package, the whole works. A beautiful gun, still in the original factory wrapping. *The damned thing had a barrel eight and three eighths inches long!* A damned *howitzer*! Hardly inconspicuous...his new cannon was too big for Dirty Harry to lug around! But the guy had made Arnold a terrific deal, and so he scooped it up.

"Arnold was *so* proud of his pet cannon, and he was too big and tough to joke around with. He didn't know how to work it, so I volunteered to go out with him and teach him to shoot. I've never been known for my intelligence...

"We drove to 'the tree' on Paris Road...the unofficial Sheriff's Office shooting range in those days. We went out there in Arnold's car, which he shared with his wife. We arrived and got out the guns...Arnold's big shiny new .357 Magnum bazooka, and I was going to fire my old .45 automatic.

"I showed Arnold how to open the cylinder, load in the cartridges, close the cylinder, and how the single-action and double-action modes worked. Finally, I taught him how to look through the sights. I had him bring a cardboard box to shoot at, and Arnold went out and set it up.

"I put in my earplugs and watched Arnold. He was going to be using the hottest .357 Magnum loads the local gun shop carried. I had advised him to use the cheaper .38 Special wadcutters to practice with, but Arnold was a macho man, and he wanted the meanest stuff he could get. After checking that there was no danger to anyone, I nodded and Arnold started firing eagerly at the box. He seemed to be doing okay, so I started popping away with my pistol.

"Now, I have to admit that I wasn't really paying much attention to Arnold, I was having too much fun shooting at cans by the tree. I fired several magazines' worth of reloads and finished shooting, so I started watching Arnold.

"Arnold was doing pretty well...firing all six shots, opening the cylinder and ejecting the fired cases, and snapping in new cartridges with a HKS speedloader. He was shooting the box to pieces, having a great time.

"Understand that Arnold was leaning across the hood of his car as he fired. He was shooting *through* it! With his sight perspective, he thought he was shootiing over it... an optical illusion. But the trajectory of his bullets brought them through the top of the hood and out the right-hand fender...I could see big blossoms of torn steel open as the bullets blasted through the fender.

"I tried to get Arnold's attention, but he waved me away with an irritated look. I pointed at the shot up hood and fender, but he just ignored me with a glare. I started laughing, and couldn't stop. I was literally holding my sides, damned near hysterical, laughing at the giant shooting his car to pieces. Of course, I wasn't an idiot, I had moved back so he couldn't *see* me laughing at him.

"Finally, Arnold ran out of ammunition, which made me feel a little better. He might beat me to death with his big revolver, but now he couldn't shoot me with it. He took out his ear plugs and turned to see me still laughing like a fool. I told him, "Arnold, I tried to tell you... but you were just shooting Hell out of your car!' Arnold bounded over to the far side of his car and you should have seen his face...

"Well, we made a little scene out there that day, but we're still friends. I never went shooting with him again, though. (*Grin*)

"But I'll never forget the weird sounds the wind made as it whistled through the new holes in the hood and fender, as we drove back to the station..." (Deputy Sheriff)

> *"Humor is emotional chaos remembered in tranquility."*
>
> *(James Thurber)*

CURIOSITY

"I used to spend a lot of time in the Orleans Parish Morgue on South White Street. We brought them a lot of business. I used to enjoy opening the stainless steel doors in the refrigerated storage room and pulling out the steel trays, examining the corpses and wondering how they died. Usually it was pretty obvious... bad wrecks, drownings, stabbings, shooting victims... they all come to the Morgue.

"Once, I pulled out a drawer and it contained a large plastic bag of what appeared to be ground beef. A pretty large quantity of it, too. I surmised that one of the Morgue employees had pet dogs at home and kept the meat fresh for them here, where it's always cool. Perhaps the guy didn't have a refrigerator at home, or it was filled with otherr things. Anyway, it didn't concern me, and I was pushing the drawer back in when I saw them... the human teeth. And then the long bones. *I was looking at human remains!*

"I was shocked, to say the least. The body wasn't in the regulation heavy zippered black plastic bag, like they usually use. I realized that the body had been immersed in water for a very long time, and I shut that drawer fast, let me tell you. I backed away, rubbing my hands on my pants...

"The guy in the office told me that the 'body' had been fished out of the Mississippi River, where it had been for perhaps six months. That little incident cured me of my curiosity at the City Morgue... at least for a while." (Deputy Sheriff)

"Curiosity is one of the most permanent and certain characteristics of a vigorous intellect."
(Dr. Samuel Johnson)

THE E.M.T.

"We got a Code 3 call about a man hurt on a ship up in Arabi. Hurt bad. We rolled on it, a heavy Code 3... Larry Ingargiola and myself. We got to the ship with all our medial gear and went aboard fast. By the looks on the crew's faces, we knew it was a bad one. It was...

"Our patient had been working near a power winch and somehow his foot got tangled in it. The winch got his foot and started crushing it. It began pulling his leg in, too...it ripped the man's leg off, leaving a horrible, jagged wound that opened him from his scrotum to just under his armpit. Imagine how that *feels*...your leg slowly twisted, crushed, and torn off, and knowing there's not a damned thing you can do about it...

"The victim was lying on the deck with this massive wound, blood everywhere, deeply in shock, other crew members muttering, and some of them cursing. We went right to work...I got on the radio and called the entire world. Trying to coordinate the rescue... We had to stabilize this guy, get him transported off the ship into our module somehow, and treat him *en route* to the hospital.

Larry was great...the consummate EMT. He got the guy positioned properly and started intravenous drips everywhere he could get a needle into a vein. I was pushing *handfuls* of ABD (abdominal) pads into the wound... I used every pad in the module. I started him on 100 percent oxygen and put blood pressure cuffs on the IV bags so we could force fluids into the patient; his circulatory system volume was *way* down.

"As we're doing all this, we're packaging him for transport. The ship's crew was great...we didn't speak a word of their language, and none of them spoke English. It didn't matter...we just *pointed* at something, and it was done instantly. Those guys were wonderful.

"We lifted the man across to the dock with a crane, loaded him into the module, and began transporting him to the nearest hospital. We worked like madmen the whole trip...a regular street Deputy drove the module and, God Bless him, he was cool and experienced enough to drive fast but *smoothly*...so he didn't toss us around in back and ruin our efforts.

"I'd already made radio contact with the E.R. Physician and gave him the data on the patient. The physician raised Hell with me for not trying to rescue the leg, but I ignored him...I'd seen it in the winch and knew it was unsalvageable. It was nothing but ripped tissue and shattered bone fragments...

"We got our patient to the Emergency Room at Chalmette General and continued our efforts for hours. We lost him... just too much trauma, too much insult to the body. One thing I'll *never* forget, though... I still find it hard to deal with. I've never told anyone this before...

"At one point while we were working, sometimes you get so busy you tend to forget that you're working on a complete *human being* instead of just juggling a complex set of problems, most of which need immediate attention. He, the patient, put his hand on my arm. I took the time to *look* at him. At his face. He had a gentle kind of smile. He *knew* he was dying, but he was thanking us for our help. He knew we were doing our very best.

"He knew we had done as much as anyone, any people, could do. I felt so helpless that I couldn't do more to save him. So much frustration; and some guilt. Unworthy to be witnessing the man's final moments of life, which should have been shared with his friends or family. His loved ones, instead of foreign strangers. The man sensed this; and, with that little smile, and that *look* in his eyes, I know he knew what I was feeling, and he let me...us...off the hook. *I'll never forget that man, not as long as I live."* (Author's experience)

> *"Nothing that was worthy in the past departs; no truth or goodness realized by man ever dies, or can die."*
>
> *(Thomas Carlyle)*

GHOST CALLER

"It was only six-thirty or so in the morning; we had just gone on duty for the day watch. I was working in the Radio room, and received a call on the 911 system. I asked what the nature of the emergency was: police, fire or medical. All I heard was static on the line. I again asked the caller what the nature of the emergency was...but still got nothing but static. On the 911 screen display, it gave an address and a name, so I held the line and dispatched a road deputy to check out the problem.

"The deputy arrived and called in immediately. "Headquarters, this is a bad call. There isn't a house at this address...not anymore. It's burned down. As a matter of fact, it burned down some time ago."

"Now, I was still holding the line, hearing static, which was all being tape-recorded. The screen still displayed the caller's name and address. I asked the deputy to verify the address, and it all checked out.

"The deputy radioed back in, "Headquarters, all the phone lines going to that address are gone. They're burned away and just hanging 'bout thirty feet in the air, still attached to the utility pole. Even the power lines are melted and burned away."

"I called my rank and informed him of the unusual situation, and he told me, "Have the deputy stand by at that address while you get a 911 troubleshooting team to go out there and clear up the problem."

"A short time later, the deputy radioed back that the 911 team had arrived and were checking out the lines in the system.

They never did find out how the call had originated at that address. Probably some kind of weird bug in the system software, but no one really knows.

"By the way, I found out later, from another dispatcher, that that house fire was a fatality incident. The occupant, an old woman who lived alone, had died from smoke inhalation, near the back of the house. They found her with her telephone still in her hand. Real *Twilight Zone* material, but it actually happened." (Deputy Sheriff)

> *"We often congratulate ourselves at the moment of waking from a troubled dream; it may be so at the moment of death."*
>
> *(Nathaniel Hawthorne)*

OLD GENTILLY

"Around 1978, I was domiciled at an apartment at 13501 Chef Menteur Highway in New Orleans East. I was employed as a Deputy Sheriff/EMT with the St. Bernard Parish Sheriff's Office. They really didn't have any silly residency requirement; and, anyway, I was just minutes away from work.

"One nasty winter evening...it had been raining all day, I had my girlfriend over. I was showing her how to operate my modest amateur radio station.

"All of a sudden, the power snapped off! As a matter of fact, every light in the apartment complex went out. It suddenly went eerily silent, as all my neighbors' televisions and stereos went out, too.

"I looked outside...I lived on the third floor...and I saw that there were no lights as far as I could see. Not good.

"I decided to cut the evening short and take my girlfriend back to her home, in Arabi. I knew better than to take Chef Mentaur Highway; with the power outage, all the traffic signals would be out. That would quickly become a nightmare, so I chose Old Gentilly Road, which had no traffic signals to bother with, anyway. I'd take it and work over to Paris Road.

"As we proceeded along Old Gentilly, I looked left at an incredible lightshow... showers of intense sparks raining down from a damaged metal utility pole, lighting up the entire area. I saw a fresh hole in the roadside chain-link fence and muddy ruts leading out into the swampy ground.

"I pulled over, put my emergency flashers on, and rolled down my window. I could see a car stuck out there, too, about fifty yards out in the swampy muck. It appeared that the driver had lost control of his vehicle, left the roadway, punched through the fence, and then smacked the metal utility pole with enough force to knock some wires loose.

"Well, that solved the mystery of the power outage...

"I asked my girlfriend to sit tight. I told her that I was going to check the car, in case someone was still in it. After all, I didn't see any footprints out in the mud.

"I slogged through the mud and muck. Finally, I arrived at the car. Its front end was pretty banged up. A white male was still behind the wheel, moaning and covered with blood. He was unconscious. So I had to somehow wake him up and see if he could walk, or carry him out myself...

"Understand that it was showering drops of molten metal. Those beautiful flashes took their toll. I really wanted the guy to walk or run out with me, to get away pronto. Those damned things *hurt!*

"I looked back, to where I had parked my car, and saw that other vehicles were stopping, too. Thank God for passers by!

"The driver, in the car, was breathing okay. I couldn't see any obvious injuries, but he just wouldn't wake up. I finally hustled him out of his door window. The door was jammed shut from the impact. All the window glass was gone, and easing him through the window wasn't too difficult...

"I hoisted him in the standard Fireman's Carry, but he was pretty hefty. That mud was slippery, as well as deep. I kept falling down. I finally elected to just drag him clear of the area and the rain of molten metal drops.

"Suddenly, I had help... two of the passers-by had seen my difficulties, and they slogged out to help, too. Thank God!

"We were making pretty good progress back to the roadway, but, suddenly, there was a *tremendous* explosion overhead...it was *deafening!* All of us were knocked over. What a night this was turning out to be...

"When I finally got to my feet, I saw that my two new 'helpers' left me alone with the injured driver.

"Well, thanks for what you did, gentlemen!

"Here, the footing was better. I finally hoisted the guy

onto my shoulder and made it to the dry roadway, where I carefully put him down.

"I was trying to check my patient when an NOPD EMS unit pulled up, blue lights flashing.

HOORAY!

"The two NOPD guys took over. We packaged up the injured driver, placed him in the EMS unit, and they hustled him off to Methodist Hospital's Emergency Room.

"I took my girlfriend home...she was miffed...and she ended our relationship.

"I went back to my apartment and calmed down as I tried to clean up.

"I was a ball of mud, which was a blessing. Those sparks and the drops of molten metal had burned dozens of holes in my heavy leather flight jacket, and I discovered quite a few fresh wounds in my hair and skin. The mud had protected me more than I had realized.

"I took a shower by candle-light, and then telephoned St. Bernard Sheriff's Office Communications. I had them punch a time and item number, so I could submit an incident report.

"At the scene, I had informed the NOPD guys that I was a deputy sheriff/EMT, so they jotted down all my identifying information down for *their* report.

"I was informed that the two NOPD guys had been awarded Lifesaving Medals, and that the injured driver had succumbed to his injuries...

"As for *me*, I lost a girlfriend, a damned good flight jacket, picked up some neat new scars, and had an interesting night. I also got a *thorough* ass-chewing from my rank for getting involved in something that was none of my business. C'est la vie!" (Author's experience)

"No good deed ever goes unpunished."
(Timeless police and military axiom)

BLEACH

"My first day in the police academy was a blast. I'd already been a street cop for years, and I'd also served in the military, so I was able to handle the mind games. But some of the younger people, the kids, were really having a rough time.

"One of the first things they did was shove us into a classroom and give an assignment. They had a collection of little slips of paper, with a single word or common phrase written on the paper. All you had to do was get up before all those strange faces and give a five minute talk about whatever had been written on the paper. Absolutely no preparation whatsoever. Those guys clock you, too. Pal, five minutes can be an *eternity* in a situation like that. Some of those people were horrible. They really suffered up there.

"My slip of paper said, "BLEACH." When *my* turn came, I went up there and had a ball. I went into a total bullshit spiel: introduced myself, thanked the people for their kind attention, and went into a tirade about the glories of bleach, its history, uses, benefits to mankind, (laughing), I even drew a 'chemical diagram' on the blackboard...some total bullshit I improvised on the spot. I fielded questions from my 'audience.' The academy instructors, I hadn't fooled them one bit, those guys were grinning their asses off. They damned near had to drag me away. I was really on a roll.

"Their object was to get the group of strangers together and break the ice. Nothing makes faster friends than a common enemy. And they really wanted to see how we could improvise in an unfamiliar environment. You know, those thinking-on-your-feet situations a street cop has to contend with. They wanted to assess this quality in us. The bullshit factor. All *good* street cops are natural bullshit artists. Usually it's not so much *what* you say as *how* you say it, your presentation." (Police Officer)

"All the animals except man know that the principle business of life is to enjoy it."
(Samuel Butler)

COOL DRINK

"We were doing a sex crime investigation in the city. We'd developed some good evidence, got a warrant signed, and hit this college professor's home. The professor didn't seem to care much about what we did or what we found. He had some 'heavy' friends downtown, and all of us knew it.

"We found an official FFA (Fist Fuckers of America) recruiting video and some real impedimenta: bondage and discipline masks and tables, rubber toys, leather garments, an honest-to-God rack, videotapes, books and magazines, weird lubricants, nipple clamps, handcuffs, you name it. He had a really terrific collection of whips, too. The professor even had an impressive array of material from NAMBLA, the North American Man-Boy Love Association.

"One of our uniform guys asked me to come into the kitchen and take a look in the refrigerator. He'd seen something unusual and wanted me to take a look at it. He wanted my opinion. I went over to the 'fridge, opened it, looked in, winced, and asked the professor to come over and tell us what it was. I already knew, but I wanted him to confirm it.

"Yes, it's semen, sperm to you people. Human sperm.." He had better than a dozen bottles of this stuff in there!

"I'm like any other guy," he went on. "Sometimes I like to get up in the middle of the night, and get something cool to drink."

I wanted to kill the asshole right then and there; but, that wouldn't have solved the problem." (Detective)

"Justice is too good for some people, and not good enough for the rest."
(Norman Douglas)

TROOPER

"We had a Louisiana State Trooper that used to work in the Parish. Jack Harrison, B-53, a huge guy, really professional, and a nice guy, too. He didn't take *any* crap, though. He was one tough son of a gun.

"One night, we had a fight break out on St. Bernard

Highway, below Paris Road. A barroom brawl. Actually, it was a small riot. They were even outside in the parking lot duking it out when we rolled up. It was just like in the movies!

"Jack was already there kicking ass. He was having *fun.* Anyway, my partner and I bailed out and got into the thick of it ourselves. We were using our fists, I didn't even *have* a baton or a slap jack back then.

"At one point, I took a swing at some asshole. I put my whole arm and shoulder into that punch, because I wanted him to *feel* it. The guy ducked and I popped Jack right in the face! Broke his glasses and *really* pissed him *off.*

"Anyway, we got the brawl under control and started putting people in jail. Jack developed a really beautiful black eye. He wouldn't speak to me for *weeks."* (Deputy Sheriff)

> *"I do not believe that friends are necessarily the people you like best, they are merely the people who got there first."*
>
> *(Peter Ustinov)*

THE DEFECTIVE DETECTIVE

"We got a call about a Signal 20-I (accident with injury) on St. Bernard Highway by Norton Avenue. A man down in the street, a possible hit-and-run victim. We rolled Code 3. We got to the scene fast. I jumped out to examine the injured man.

"He was rolling around in the street, screaming. He wouldn't stay still so I could examine him. He kept saying, "I'm dying... I'm dying." Seconds later, he went still and stopped breathing. I tore open his shirt to start CPR. I saw them then...the wounds. The man had been shot with a shotgun. He died on the scene.

"Later, during the investigation on the scene, we were all searching for physical evidence. One of my colleagues found a shotgun lying in the ditch just south of the highway, about sixty feet from the dead man. The deputy didn't touch the shotgun, but he called my attention to it, and I summoned our detectives.

"The detectives came right over. One of them stepped down near the water and picked up the shotgun. He didn't mark the area, or photograph the scene. He just picked up the gun and starting running his hands all over it. I guess he'd never heard of fingerprints?

"His examination of the weapon consisted of sniffing the muzzle, running his hands all over the barrel and stock, and then, finally, opening the action. A spent 12-gauge hull was ejected. It landed in the ditch and sank in the muddy water. The 'detective' *ignored it*. He said it "wasn't significant to the investigation." Can you believe that? Right then I left the scene. I couldn't believe how amateurishly the 'detective' was handling the case. I didn't want to be a party to it. I didn't want to be a witness to this bullshit. They never did catch the killer, of course. I guess they didn't want to. After all, this is St. Bernard Parish, not the *real* world." (Deputy Sheriff)

"A person can only be murdered once, but a crime scene can be murdered a thousand times."
(Police Axiom)

RADIO SEX

"One night, we were working the evening shift, and had been pretty busy most of the time. A little after ten P.M. or so, it started to calm down a little. We were en route to a minor complaint call when our police radio started making...weird sounds. We didn't have portable radios, just the ones installed in the patrol cars.

"The sounds on the radio came from a couple who were screwing their brains out! The couple was grinding away, boy, and moaning and groaning. It was so *clear*. My partner and I looked at each other in amazement, then we started laughing. We really 'lost it.' We had to pull off the road to avoid an accident. We laughed so hard we *cried.*

"Apparently, this deputy and his 'lady love' got involved, and inadvertently keyed up the vehicle's radio transmitter. They were actually having intercourse atop the microphone somehow. The dummy was one of those guys who never used the microphone hanger thing on the dashboard, he just tossed the microphone on the seat.

"We couldn't help the idiots, not even the Radio Room could override their transmission. The dispatcher enjoyed the action at first, but started getting pissed when their phones started lighting up. People at home monitoring their scanners were going *nuts*.

"Their broadcast continued for nearly *twenty minutes!* We just sat there, grinning and enjoying the entertainment. We knew who the guilty party was, we recognized their voices. We envied the deputy and his 'lady' for having such a great time. We gleefully anticipated their shock when they discovered that they'd been 'on the air' for most of their rendezvous." (Deputy Sheriff)

"Sex, unlike justice, should not be seen to be done."
(Evelyn Laye)

JUST PRACTICING

"We saw a parked car just off Patricia Street behind Sidney Torres Park. The windows were fogged up, so we had a good hunch what was going on inside. We got out of the patrol unit and approached the car, announcing ourselves as the police...

"We lit up the car with our flashlights, so we could see what was happening inside. We wanted the odds in *our* favor. Sometimes, a woman is abducted and raped, and we wanted to make damned sure that wasn't happening here. Sure enough, there was a couple in the car...a man and a woman. They were still breathing hard and perspiring heavily.

"That was easy to see, since both of them were buck-assed naked. There was *no* doubt they'd been going at it hot and heavy. The guy looked nervous and scared, but the woman...and she was *all* woman, if you know what I mean, she just sat up, all proud of herself. She said, "It's okay, Officers. We're gettin' married next week and we were just practicing for the honeymoon." (Deputy Sheriff)

"We were just necking, Officer." "Yessir, I can see that. Tell you what, Cap. Why don't you put your 'neck' back in your pants, zip 'em up, and you two gentlemen get out of here?" (Police Officer)

MAGGOTS

"We were asked to check a house for a possible Signal 29, a dead body. My partner was a young kid, but he seemed to be pretty good. We rolled over to the address they'd given us, and got out to see what we could find. I was hoping it was a dead body call, because I wanted to see how the new kid would handle his first stinker call.

"The house looked like it was vacant, but had been lived in by dope-fiends. You know, run-down looking, high grass, painted out windows, the works. No one was around to give us any information, but then no one ever did in that sector. It was after nine P.M., pitch dark, but we had a job to do.

"We walked up to the front door, carefully announced ourselves as the police, and went on in. The front door was open. My partner didn't yet have a flashlight, and mine was cranky. It worked when *it* wanted to. I reached around for the light switch and clicked it several times...but no lights. *Big* surprise. My partner, the eager beaver, stumbled his way deeper into the stinking house as I tried to get my big, rechargeable flashlight working. I cussed the damned thing...nearly a hundred bucks for the son of a gun, and it was a lemon. *Piss on it!*

"I followed my partner into the filthy interior of the old house. It smelled *very* bad. I had no problem believing *something* had died in here. I was till pounding on my flashlight, trying to get it operating, becuse I was bumping into furniture and junk. Shortly, I heard weird *crunching* noises beneath my boots. Apparently, vandals had been rummaging around in the house, and had tossed corn flakes all over the floor.

"Suddenly, my partner started *screaming* his ass off, so I grabbed my portable radio and broadcast our number and "108!" our "officer needs assistance" code. My partner was still screaming and struggling with *someone* in the next room. I could hear the thumps as they were hitting each other. I guessed my partner had run into a crazy dope-fiend, so I was trying desperately to get in there and help him. I pulled my Smith & Wesson Model 66 revolver. My partner and his assailant were smashing into walls...I heard screaming, thuds, weird noises, then breaking glass. If only my goddamned flashlight *worked!*

"Excited and in a frenzy to assist my partner, I bumped into something hard, and dropped my flashlight, but held on to my revolver. I heard my partner cry out again, and it sounded like he'd gotten further away from me, still crashing and thumping against the walls as he fought desperately with the crazed dope-fiend. Dammit, it was so dark in there, it was pitch black...I couldn't even see my own hands. Then I bumped into something else and toppled over, dropping my Smith & Wesson and sort of sliding along on the floor, which was wet and slippery. And it was crunchier than ever. What the hell?

"District cars zoomed up outside. I thought, *"The Cavalry has arrived!"* Then I heard anxious voices, then laughs. *Laughs?* I heard someone put a Code 4 over the air. They were laughing outside, laughing hysterically. Suddenly, I could *see*...a blinding white beam struck me from the next room. My buddies had gotten to me! One of them said, "Come on out here, asshole!" as he held me in the beam of light. I could see his grin in the light's backscatter. I instinctively reached down for my Smith & Wesson...and then I didn't want it. I wanted OUT! The things covering my gun, and my boots...the crunching sounds...*MAGGOTS!* Millions of *MAGGOTS!* I escaped from the room, ran through the house, and made it to clean outside air. I wanted to tear my uniform off. I wanted a hot shower. Goddamned *maggots*...I wanted to tear my skin off and burn it.

"My partner was outside, too, wide-eyed, nearly naked, and very shook up. I got the story. My partner had found the dead body, an old wino, by *falling* onto, no, *into* him in the darkness, when he slipped on the maggot-covered floor. He freaked out, screaming, fighting to get away from the rotting old wino, who had broken apart when the kid had toppled into him...nasty chunks of the rotting wino were stuck and 'glued' to him! He was retching from the incredibly foul stench, bouncing off everything, and had finally toppled into one of the painted-out windows and shattered it, falling outside. He wasn't injured, but he was definitely worked up and sick, vomiting his guts out.

"I went back inside and retrieved my Model 66. I didn't want to, but I *had* to. I left the cantankerous flashlight in there. It's probably still there today...you can have it, if you want.

"I threw away my nasty uniform, my boots, even my underwear. And, I bought another flashlight the next day...one that *worked*. And I still don't think I deserve the nickname those assholes gave me." (Police Officer)

"A wise man sees as much as he ought, not as much as he can."

(Michel de Montaigne)

KANINNY

"I was working light duty in the Radio Room. Some guy called the Sheriff's Office and wanted to make a complaint about a deputy who was driving around in a squad car with a dog in the back seat. He thought it was cruel to the dog to make it sit in the car. He thought it was unsanitary for the prisoners, too. I realized that the caller was an idiot.

"Then he *confirmed* it. "The deputy's name is "Kaninny," he told me. That's how he pronounced it, "Kuh-ninny." We didn't *have* any deputies named Kaninny, but I wanted this bullshit on tape...all the calls are taped.

"I suddenly had a hunch, I just *knew* what was coming next, so I asked him, "Sir, can I ask you where you got that name?" He goes, "Sure. He painted it right there on the side of the squad car, in red letters..."C A N I N E." (Deputy Sheriff)

> *"He was born stupid, and greatly increased his birthright."*
>
> *(Samuel Butler)*

OOPS!

"I drove by Kelly, my partner's house, to pick him up. We were working a plain clothes detail. I tapped the horn, and Kelly, expecting me, appeared in the door and waved to me. He disappeared back inside. Seconds later I heard a gunshot, then angry voices. I thought, "*Now what the fuck was that all about?"*

"This is what had happened...Kelly had gone back in to get his pistol. He'd just bought a brand-new Colt "Combat Commander" in .45 ACP. One of those satin nickel ones. He'd only had it two days, and was really proud of it. He kept it in his bedroom, next to the bed. Kelly kept it unloaded, because his wife,

Cathy, was scared of firearms and insisted on the gun being unloaded before he brought it inside.

"Kelly had walked into the bedroom, kissed Cathy, grabbed his new .45 pistol, inserted a loaded magazine, and then 'jacked' the slide, chambering a cartridge. In a little bit of a hurry, Kelly *tried* to lower the hammer with his thumb, but...it slipped.

"BOOM!"

"Kelly accidentally managed to blast a nice .45 caliber hole into his pillow, just about a foot from Cathy's head. Cathy was *pissed*.

"Kelly sold me his "Combat Commander" that same night...for a hundred bucks." (Detective)

> *"I have never seen a stiuation so dismal that a policeman couldn't make it worse."*
> *(Brendan Behan)*

THE KILLER BUSH

"I was new on the street, very energetic, badge-heavy, and overbearing...what they call a "robocop" nowadays. I jumped every call that came out. I was really eager to prove myself to the older guys and make a reputation for myself as a super cop.

"Headquarters put out a 62-R (Residential Burglary) and added that it was "in progress." Talk about waving a red flag (laugh). I thought, "*Wow, a house burglary! With the burglar still inside...I can still catch him and be a hero!"*

"I *flew* to the address, but another unit was already pulling up, too. Two older deputies. My dreams of glory faded. *Oh well...*

"As I guessed, the two old farts told me to watch the back of the house while they checked the front. They'd flush the burglar out to me. I thought, "*Yeah, right!"* So I went to the back of the house, which had a high wooden fence. Damned thing was over six feet tall! I was still incredibly stupid, so I intended to vault over the fence and be ready to catch the burglar. I'd show the older deputies I was pretty tough, and capable of anything it took to get the job done.

"So, I took a running start and jumped onto the fence, easily pulling myself up and over the top..."*Zing! Oh, I am so cool! I'm just like Batman!"* I sailed over the top of the fence and landed on a fuckin' Yucca plant...you know, one of those bushes that is nothing but a bunch of leaves like knife blades...just needle-tipped leaves?

"I couldn't help screaming as the leaves stabbed me. They *really* hurt. I actually thought I was being killed. Anyway, the older deputies heard all the yelling, and thought I was fighting with the burglar in the back yard. They 'John Wayned'd' (kicked in) the front door and rushed out to help me...but finding me in the back yard getting my ass kicked by a *plant.*

"They laughed their behinds off, but helped get me out of the "killer bush" and got me patched up. We never did catch the burglar; and, as it turned out, it was just a glitch in the alarm system...the only break-in at that address was the one *we* perpetrated. But we all learned a valuable lesson that evening. *Me most of all.*" (Deputy Sheriff)

"Man is the only animal that blushes. Or needs to."
(Mark Twain)

THE TOURIST

'One day, we were just crusing through the French Quarter listening to music on the squad car's old AM radio. We were taking a 'short cut' back to the district on North Rampart. Some poor soul, obviously lost, beckoned to us. My partner, Eddie, a real character, pulled over so the guy could talk to us. The poor soul looked like a dipshit, and we really weren't in the mood to listen to whatever bullshit story he was going to throw at us. It was such a *pretty* day to waste on an asshole, y'know what I mean?

"Anyway, the dipshit guy asked for an obscure address, and old Eddie, well, he brightened up. *Mr. Nice Guy*. He gave complete, thorough, detailed directions to the bedazzled dipshit. Totally *wrong* directions, but I didn't interfere. It was just too good to spoil. Finally, the dipshit thanked us, shook our hands, beamed at us, and went his merry way, faithful to Eddie's bullshit directions.

"Smirking, I told Eddie, "You asshole! In about three minutes, he's gonna be swimming in the River, with those asinine directions you gave him."

"Eddie looked at me, grinned, then laughed. "Yeah, I know," he said, clearly delighted with his cruel prank, "But, *fuck* him. He's a *tourist*!" (Police Officer)

"The vagabond, when rich, is called a tourist."
(Paul Richard)

GEORGE THE TROOPER

"George Lupo, Louisiana State Trooper, was assigned to Troop "B," but he worked mainly in St. Bernard Parish when I knew him. He was a very quiet, very professional, no-nonsense cop. A former Marine. It showed, too. He wasn't a big guy, but he was a big man. He was 99 percent *balls*. He was fair and reasonable, but his word was law.

"One night, the Radio Room started getting frantic calls for help in Violet. People in Violet (a small town "down the road") were complaining that the Louisiana State Police were "attacking" them. The State Troopers were brutalizing the "Vio-la-tions" *(I know, it sounds like 'violations'.)* All sorts of crazy bullshit; the people in the Radio Room were going nuts.

"It sounded interesting, so we rolled down there to see what was actually happening. The "Violations" were quite correct... The State Police *were* attacking them. It was George the Trooper... all by himself. *We loved it.*

"Some dumbass got pulled over by George. Instead of taking his citations like a man, or going to jail, the fool decided to escape into Violet. He was only a couple of blocks from his house, where all his buddies were hanging in the bars anyway. So there was *no way* that State Trooper was going to get *him*.

"He was wrong. George *did* get him. In a professional manner, but he got him. Never before or since have the Louisiana State Police been accorded the absolute respect George earned that night. He was *awesome.* You remember the old Texas Ranger motto..., "One Riot, One Ranger?" George Lupo was that kind of Trooper. *Those* were the good old days." (Deputy Sheriff)

> *Resistance to the organized mass can be effected only by the man who is as well organized in his individuality as the mass itself."*
>
> *(Carl Jung)*

REPUTATION

"I used to work with a guy that had a *horrible* reputation on the street. I was afraid to work with him, at first. You know, the psycho Vietnam veteran who tortures little kids, eats raw meat, all that bullshit. Hell, I believed it myself...but after working with him a few tours, I saw that it was all bullshit. Let's call him "Joe" because I don't want to embarrass him.

"Joe was an excellent policeman. He gave terrific service to the citizens, never bad mouthed them, never even put his hands on them, if he could avoid it. He was a fantastic cop and a really nice person, once you got to know him. Joe didn't let his shield down much, though. He was a very private guy, but I knew that he'd open up to me, after I had earned his trust.

"It bothered me that people thought of him in such a negative light. I asked him about it. He laughed, but curtly told me to mind my own business...his reputation was *his* business and no one else's. Joe did tell me, though, that he'd developed his reputation so that his enemies overestimated his faults, while his friends underestimated his good points, his positive traits. It was Joe's way of dealing with life as a street cop. Joe lived by his own rules, and his own code of ethics. Joe was a unique version of *the real police.*

"He was a great training officer and taught me a lot, both about law enforcement and about life in general.

"Joe never wanted promotions and, in fact, he refused them. He refused commendations and awards, too. He managed to live life on his own terms, not an easy thing for a member of this Department. He was quite a guy, and, to use his own phrase, he did his best to be a "*good street cop.*" Along the way, I earned the right to call him that. Being recognized as a good street policeman meant more to Joe than anything." (Deputy Sheriff)

"Show me a hero and I will write you a tragedy."
(F. Scott Fitzgerald)

TCHOUPITOULAS

"This story is so old it has *whiskers*, and it's probably the most repeated story in New Orleans, when cops start talking about "the good old days."

'One morning, a New Orleans policeman walking his beat discovered a mule, some say it was a horse, lying dead at the intersection of Tchoupitoulas and Common Streets. As usual, the policeman had some paperwork to do.

"He took out his little notebook, to jot down the particulars, and realized that he couldn't *spell* the word "Tchoupitoulas." Scratching his head, he looked around, trying to get inspiration. The usual street sign was long gone.

"Finally, the policeman gave up, grabbed the dead mule by the tail, and dragged it a whole city block! Sweating and exhausted, the pliceman dug out his notebook and wrote, "Dead mule found in the street at Magazine and Common." (Police Officer)

> *"It's not what you do in this life that counts...it's what people think you do. And that can be good or bad."*
>
> *(Author)*

STATE OF INTOXICATION

"One night, we handled a serious Signal 20-I (accident with injury) at the end of Judge Perez Drive (State Highway 39). In those days, Judge Perez ended at Colonial Boulevard. At its end was a few feet of concrete lined with traffic cones, and numerous warning signs.

"Behind the traffic cones and the warning signs, which were often stolen, was yet another row of barricades, with reflectors and flashing yellow winky lights, more concrete, then the actual end of the road...a high wooden barrier painted orange-and-white, with reflective strips and more flashing yellow lights. There was *no way* you couldn't realize that you had reached the end of the road. But people crashed into the barriers all the time.

"A drunk lawyer and his girlfriend, who was married but not to *him*, zoomed through the cones, the signs, the barricades, and rocketed into the final wooden barrier. Smashing through the barrier, their car finally smacked into a large tree about sixty feet behind the barrier. They were pretty badly injured, as you can imagine.

"The lawyer had both legs broken and several cracked ribs, and he'd lost several teeth. The woman had fared a little better, but still suffered numerous fractures. As you can imagine, there was blood and shattered glass everywhere. It was a real mess.

"Some kind soul witnessed the crash and phoned the Sheriff's Office. When we got there, we had a hard time *finding* the car back there in the dark, dense woods, but we soon found it and the moaning victims.

"But the lawyer's first comment was the *really* memorable thing from the incident. The man is lying there in his wrecked car, blood and glass everywhere, his lady companion moaning in pain. He was badly injured and in considerable pain himself...the effects of the booze were wearing off fast.

"He's spitting out bits of broken teeth, coughing up blood, and vomiting, but he still had a *little* bit of dignity left. When we emerged from the darkness to help them, the lawyer's glazed eyes locked onto our uniforms, patches and badges. They were obviously unfamiliar to him. Coughing a bit, the bewildered lawyer asked us, "Are you guys the Gulfport Police?"

"We didn't have the heart to tell him how far off course he was. *Gulfport is on the Mississippi Gulf Coast...ninety miles away."* (Deputy Sheriff)

> *"I may not here omit those two main plagues, and common dotages of human kind, wine and women, which have often infatuated and besotted myriads*

of people. They go commonly together."
(Robert Burton)

PLEASE CUT HER FINGERS OFF...

"I got a call from one of our regular deputies who worked the evening shift. He asked me to come over to his house...and not to use my lights or siren. He didn't want any attention. I drove to his house. He let me in quietly, his finger to his lips in the classic 'Shhhhh'...

"On the couch in the living room was his wife. She was dead...as a matter of fact, she was *very* dead. Rigor mortis was fully developed. She exhibited post-mortem lividity in all the lower portions of her anatomy. These were areas where the blood pooled up, after the heart stopped circulating it. Gravity makes it settle in the lowest parts of the body. From her position and the areas of the lividity, I knew she had died right where she was.

"She'd been watching her beloved soap operas on television. The old lady had some severe medical problems she'd suffered with for many years, so I had no reason to suspect foul play. By the way, I found out later, after the autopsy, that she *had* died a natural death.

"But the deputy had been gone all night and day, leaving the old lady all alone. He worked as a 'night watchman' which meant that he mostly slept at night, and, days, he worked at the railroad, not sure what he did there. And, in the evenings, he played police with the sheriff's office.

"You know what that asshole wanted me to do? He wanted *me* to get his wife's rings. She was wearing some expensive ones when she died. He wanted to get her rings off, so he could give them to his girlfriend. He didn't want me to use a ring-cutter on the rings, since that might spoil them. He asked me to just "cut her fingers off." He couldn't do it, but he thought *I* could. He wanted to clean up the rings and present them to his girlfriend later that night. That sick bastard...

"I told him, "You go fuck yourself!" I left his house and never spoke to him again." (Deputy Sheriff)

> *"Avarice is generally the last passion of those lives, of which the first part has been squandered in pleasure, and the second devoted to ambition."*
> *(Dr. Samuel Johnson)*

PYTHON

"Some cops are idiots, which complicates life for themselves, other cops, and the public we attempt to serve. We got saddled with a guy from a State agency...he was one of those spit-and-polish, rigidly 'by the book' screwballs with not a whit of common sense.

"He was fastidious, I'll give him that. He was also peculiarly attached to his nickel-plated 4-inch Colt Python, which he had had buffed out. He could *barely* qualify with it, but he spent hours cleaning it, polishing it, and caressing it.

"One of his former colleagues confided in us one afternoon. He told us this guy's story...

"One bright and sunny afternoon, our hero had made a traffic stop on the Bridge. He went up to the driver, all smiling and carefree and confident of his brilliant smile and pleasant demeanor. Everyone just loved him.

"The driver of the stopped vehicle had instantly produced a revolver and started firing at our new officer!

"Our boy just stood there, mouth agape, as the driver popped at him from point-blank range. His uniform actually caught fire as tiny bits of burning gunpowder was blasted into it. The shooter successfully shot one of his shoulder patches off his uniform!

"Our new officer had just stood there...frozen, as the guy emptied his revolver and then, casually departed the scene. He just drove away quietly...no rush...no big deal...

"Witnesses freaked at the bizarre goings-on, and one of them called in to report that a policeman was being shot at atop the Bridge. Our new guy hadn't even called in the traffic stop, so no one was officially aware of what was going on. And the shooter made a clean getaway!

"Mind you, this was atop the Mississippi River Bridge (the old one), with traffic zooming past in both directions. An investigation revealed that our boy didn't return fire...

"The reason, you ask?

"Because he had just finished cleaning his Python, and he didn't want to get it dirty *unnecessarily*! He actually stated that, at the Review Board. *In front of witnesses!* Amazingly, no one had been killed or wounded...a true miracle. And his agency didn't suspend him, or impose any sort of disciplinary action whatsoever.

"After all, he had been hired under an affirmative action quota program, and he had political 'connections', so no one dared. So, in the end, *we* got stuck with this worthless asshole..." (Police Officer)

"You know, the people out here can shoot you, stick a knife in you, piss or puke on you and it's no big deal. It's us against them, and that's just the way it is...life in the big city. But what really hurts is these fuckin' politicians...the ass kissers and brown nosers. They're the ones that can really hurt you." (Police Officer)

LARRY

"Larry Ingargiola had a well-deserved reputation as an exceptionally good EMT. He put a lot of heart into his work. He was one of the original C.C.Ts...'Coronary Care Technicians', who was trained at Charity Hospital.

"In the mid-70s, before the National Registry of Emergency Medical Technicians standardized their requirements for Paramedics, being a certified C.C.T. was the highest emergency medical rating in Louisiana. Only the very best EMTs got to take the training, and Larry Ingargiola was one of them.

"One night, we received a 29-S (suicide) call. Some guy in Arabi had put a shotgun in his mouth and pulled the trigger. He was a real mess when the slot deputies responded to his address and found him. They got on the radio and started screaming for EMS on a heavy Code 3. Larry and I responded to the call, Code 3.

"When I first saw the guy, I chalked him off as a total

waste of time. Most of his face was hanging off the walls and ceiling...you could see his *brain* exposed. He wasn't breathing, which didn't come as a big shock. The deputy said he had just stopped breathing when we arrived.

"Larry elbowed me out of the way and said, "I can save him, Bo." He called *everyone* 'Bo.' He was serious, too. He got down there and started to work on the guy. We worked our asses off.

"Larry *did* save him! A big clot of jellied blood had stopped the victim's breathing, but Larry got it removed, did his medical miracles, and we got the guy to Chalmette General Hospital, where they performed major surgery. But Larry saved his life right there on the scene. It was the most incredible thing I've ever seen, the way Larry worked.

"The man was surgically repaired, but he killed himself a year or so later. The shotgun again. Ironically, the man killed himself because of his looks...he'd lost half of his face and one eye in the earlier attempt.

"But Larry Ingargiola...he was one hell of an EMT..." (Captain)

> *"Nothing great will ever be achieved without men, and men are great only if they are determined to be so."*
>
> *(Charles de Gaulle)*

BACK FROM THE DEAD

"We brought a man back from the dead once. We'd received a call from the Coast Guard about a death aboard some foreign vessel. Some seaman had died, and the ship's captain wanted him off the boat.

"The seaman had died a day or so before, and was kept in the refrigerated meat locker so he wouldn't spoil so fast. The Coast Guard told us that they'd actually get him off the ship, and deliver him onshore, but they asked us for an ambulance to take him the rest of the way to a hospital, to get him pronounced dead.

"So, we met the Coast Guard boat at the levee. They transferred the dead man to us, wrapped in a sheet. His body was cold and stiff. We didn't know what had killed the man, so we just put him in the back of the unit...an old station wagon. Both of us got in front. We didn't want to get too close to the dead guy. He might have died of some kind of disease mechanism, you know?

"We started off, with my partner driving. Now, you got to understand that my partner had never handled a corpse before. He was new to the business, and he was kind of nervous. He drove a little bit too fast; and, at one point, he actually lost control of our vehicle. We went off the road, out into a soft field, and then my partner panicked and over-corrected. We zoomed back across the road and up the levee...we nearly went over it into the River. Then he yanked the wheel to the right again. We came flying down the levee and rammed into a ditch. When we hit the ditch, we stopped... *fast*.

"TOO fast...the dead man in back got catapulted in front with us! The dead guy came over the seat like a torpedo, and scared the hell out of me. He crashed head-first into the radio console, and, so help me, he started coughing!

"He'd come back to life!

"My freaked-out, wide-eyed partner instantly ejected from his side of the wagon. And *I* was backing up along the seat, away from the animated corpse. You can't imagine how it feels, to see a dead man come to life like that. Every horror movie I'd ever seen... right there before me.

"We finally regained our composure and raced the guy to the nearest hospital. *They* saved his life.

"The doctors told me that the guy had never *really* died in the first place. He had a brain tumor and went into a coma on board the ship. His stay in the meat locker didn't really hurt him, but the timing was just right. That brutal whack on the head that we accidentally gave him did *something* to the tumor, and the guy regained consciousness. How d'ya like *that* one?" (Deputy Sheriff)

> *"Life. A spiritual pickle preserving the body from decay."*
>
> *(Ambrose Bierce)*

DOPE!

"I was working Narcotics with my partner, Mike. We'd just set up a buy out in a parking lot on Paris Road (La. 47) by Bayou Bienvenue. The guy we were going to pop was a coke dealer from Caffin Avenue in the lower Ninth Ward. I'd already shown the dealer my wad of 'flash' money, and was watching the dealer walk nonchalantly back to his car to retrieve the dope. I had just put my gun and badge down between my legs, on the seat. Mike was hovering nearby, ready to pounce.

"When the dealer handed me the dope, I showed him the badge and pistol. The dealer looked down at 'em, laughed, and pushed them out of the way.

"I said, "Police, man, you're under arrest!"

"The laughing dealer replied, "Cut the bullshit, man, 'jus gimme my money so I can gets outa here." *He thought I was joking!*

"I repeated, with some steel in my voice, "Hey, *man,* no shit, I'm the police, and you're under arrest. Don't fucking resist."

"The grinning dope dealer *still* thought I was clowning with him, but suddenly, Mike materialized beside the dealer and put the muzzle of his Smith & Wesson in the man's ear. The dealer stopped grinning and you could *see* that cold, hard reality was starting to sink in.

"The dealer realized that things were going 'downhill to shitsville' really fast. He started shaking and crying and blubbering. He was a real actor; that asshole deserved an Academy Award!

"He yelled, "Oh no....no....take the fuckin' dope...keep your fuckin' money! Take my fuckin' car! Just fuckin' lemme go!" He was starting to get *really* animated, if you know what I mean. I was watching his hands *very* closely. I don't know what he was on, but it must have been the good stuff.

"The dealer took us for ripoff artists; he thought we wanted to steal his dope. Mike 'cuffed him, and, during the pat-down search, Mike found a loaded 9mm Browning pistol stuffed in the man's dirty jeans. Another charge.

"Mike placed the dope dealer in the back seat of the transport car while I tested the dope. As it turned out, it *was* dope he'd tried to sell me, so no problems at all. Mike got in front with me, and we drove our prisoner to the Parish Jail in Chalmette. We had to drive north, up Paris Road, to make the turn around to get back to the jail.

"The dealer in back *freaked.* He thought we were going to 'dome' him (shoot him in the head) and dump his body out on Almonaster Avenue, in New Orleans East.

"Almonaster Avenue is a favorite spot for dumping murder victims.

"Before we made the turn around, the dope dealer started screaming, crying, and praying loudly. Mike said, "Hey, asshole! Just shut the fuck up and enjoy the ride. We're not going to kill you *this* time, dumbass. Mebbe *next* time, if we catch you out here in the Parish slinging shit and carrying a gun."

"That dope dealer was quiet the rest of the trip, but when we pulled into the jail's parking area, he started laughing...he was *so* happy he was only going to jail, and not to the bottom of the swamp..." (Detective)

"How did you guys find me?" the victim asked me after a dope deal went sour.

"It wasn't hard.. You left a trail of blood two blocks long."
(Author's experience)

KARMA

"Karma can be a hard-eyed bitch, but at least she deals out justice on a pretty consistent basis. One frosty night, an upstanding citizen decided to steal a car, and then added to the festivities by casually shooting at innocent people minding their own business.

"A call was put out, and in a few moments, the NOPD had something more interesting to do as we pursued the guy at white-knuckle velocities through the city as he shot at *us*, too. We coudn't shoot back at the guy, per policy, and the dictates of common sense, of course.

"The pursuit was terminated abruptly when the guy tried to jump a neutral ground and struck a small tree on Martin Luther King with such force, that the car's battery was found lying 183 feet from the point of impact. We never did find his gun; we assume a street thief ran off with it.

"The car thief/shooter was in the back seat of the smashed vehicle. He was wearing the remains of the front seat, the dashboard, and the engine in his lap, more or less. He was wheezing, choking, and bubbling blood as he tried to speak. He did manage to flip me off, defiantly, and grinned at me with his toothless mouth. All he emitted were croaking noises and a lot of 'steam' condensation into the cold air.

"I was suddenly dazzled by a sea of blue lights flashing

from all directions, and the shrieking cacophony of all those sirens, their echoes bouncing off all the hard surfaces surrounding us. Then, suddenly, it all got quiet...

"I didn't even attempt to render first aid or to extricate him. It would have been useless, anyway. I got on the radio and told the dispatcher to request that EMS knock down their response to a Code 1. This guy wasn't going to a hospital, but straight to the morgue. No use endangering them or the public to respond to a corpse. I didn't need to call for a supervisor, *everyone* was involved in this incident. I also asked them to notify the Coroner's Office...

"The dying driver was still conscious enough to hear *that* transmission. I had hoped he would. His eyes widened as it sank in. He tried to say something, but he just wheezed and bubbled...and then he was gone..." (Narcotics Agent)

> *"Experience is not what happens to a man. It is what a man does with what happens to him."*
> *(Aldous Huxley)*

FAITH

"We had a very serious accident...a fatality. A young woman got crushed in a bad car wreck. She was killed, but just *refused* to die. The EMTs had extricated her from the wreckage and got her to (name deleted) Hospital. The emergency room people did their best for her, but it was useless. Nothing they could do. The young woman's head had been crushed, and her brain was *destroyed*. It was a miracle that she was still breathing on her own.

"They placed her in one of the examining rooms and

waited for Nature to take its course. Her family was waiting outside, still in shock. She was so *young*, and such a good wife and mother. She had so much to live for...

"I got to the hospital after I'd handled the initial accident scene. When I got there, the woman was still hanging on. Since I was the shift's A.I. (accident investigator), I decided to get started on the report right there, since it was going to be a very comprehensive, detailed police report. I started my paperwork right there...just a few feet from the dying woman. It was a bad mistake...

"Every so often, she'd take these great, gasping breaths. It unnerved me. Really shook me up, because it exposed my own mortality, I guess. She was still alive, and not just a name on a piece of paper, if you get my meaning. I hurried my paperwork, trying hard to ignore her.

"After I'd gotten the report under control, I gathered it all together and put it into my clipboard. Stretching, I started talking to one of the nurses in the E.R. During the talk, the nurse remarked that the young woman just 'wouldn't give up the ghost.' I knew from the information I'd gathered, that the woman was a Roman Catholic. That got to me. I asked if her Priest had given her the Last Rites. The nurse didn't know, and eventually we discovered that no one had bothered to summon a Priest...her family was so shook up, even they had forgotten to. I guess they thought she'd be going home in a few days, that all this was just a bad dream,

"We made some quick phone calls.

"One of the local Priests, Father (name deleted) arrived promptly and started into his Priest thing, praying softly and all that. I was still pretty emotional, myself, at this point. *This one had really gotten through my armor.*

"As the Priest prayed. the woman slowly relaxed and got...peaceful, if you know what I mean. She just got all relaxed and calmed down...and...expired. She just wouldn't let go until that Priest got there... (Deputy Sheriff)

"Faith is the substance of things hoped for, the evidence of things not seen."

(The Holy Bible)

DOUBLE DROWNING

"It was getting dark on the fifth of July, the day after the big holiday. I'd been detailed to South Shore Harbor as security, when I heard over the radio that there was a possible drowning at the Seabrook Bridge, by the public boat launch. It was a popular swimming hole for the locals, especially on summer holidays. Then it got worse...it was a *double* drowning. Two little girls.

"I was the only member of the Air Sea Rescue team on duty, so my platoon commander ordered me back to Headquarters. Airport Safety took over the security detail at South Shore Harbor.

"Upon arrival at Headquarters, I gained access to our Dive Locker and started breaking out our SCUBA equipment. I assembled two sets of dive gear and was putting it into a police car when Lt. Hollard, commander of the Air Sea Rescue team, arrived from home. They'd called him in for this incident.

"We got to the scene very quickly. When we got there, it

was a circus...a giant Coast Guard helicopter was hovering overhead, churning the water with its powerful rotor blast, the noise from its twin jet engines made conversation impossible. We tried to wave it away, but they ignored us.

"The boat launch was crowded with dozens of vehicles: NOPD cars, fire department units, Harbor Police patrol cars, ambulances and paramedic units, the media, news photographers, and plain old wide-eyed, loud-mouthed rubberneckers, most of *them* with beers in their fists.

"Orleans Levee District Officers, especially Officer Ron Casse, helped us unload the dive gear and carry it to the water's edge. The Levee Board's big rescue vessel, the *Captain Lane*, was out there just north of the breakwater, making slow passes. It was equipped with side-scanning SONAR gear. A number of smaller craft from the Coast Guard and other agencies were prowling around inshore, on our side of the breakwater. It was overcast, the sun had just set, and it started to drizzle.

"As Hollard and I suited up, we got the story from witnesses. A trio of young children, two sisters and a boy, had waded into the shallow waters of the boat launch, enjoying the cool water in the afternoon's heat. None of the kids could swim. The two girls had waded out a bit further, and got into trouble...they started struggling and screaming for help, but disappeared in the murky greenish water. Some man tried to get to them, but he had problems and had to turn back. The boy was luckier, a passing boat had rescued him. People in the area started arguing about what to do, and eventually someone called the police.

"The girls' last known position was pointed out to us as we finished suiting up. We had no doubt that the girls were dead. The water's temperature was in the high 80s, and the girls had been submerged for well over an hour before we were even notified.

"I had suited up in my standard body recovery rig...a bright orange cotton coverall, full SCUBA gear, and mask and flippers. The mask leaked and the flippers were too small for me...I had had to borrow them from another diver because someone had taken *my* equipment home by mistake.

"Lt. Hollard had suited up fast, too. We were professionals, and didn't waste a lot of time. From the time we got to the scene, to the time we were entering the water, was something like four minutes. We swam out to the spot that had been pointed out to us, checked our regulators a last time, and submerged.

"Lake Pontchartrain is never pleasant to dive in, and conditions during this dive were a bit worse than usual. Visibility was less than six inches, and the sunlight was fading fast. On the bottom, it was already as dark as night, only six to eight feet down.

"Hollard and I started a standard circular search pattern, and found the first girl very quickly. She was lying peacefully on the lake's muddy bottom. I surfaced with her body, and she was taken away by one of the Coast Guard boats. Lt. Hollard had remained on the bottom, marking the position for our next search sweep. We found the other little girl in moments, resting on the bottom, just out of arms' reach of her sister..." (Author's experience)

> *"It is impossible that anything so natural, so necessary, and so universal as death should ever have been designed by Providence an evil to mankind."*

(Jonathan Swift)

THE NEW KID

"One night, I heard one of my new kids go out on a traffic stop. He had just completed his FTO training, and was working solo. We had cut him loose to see what he could do, but I was keeping a close eye on him...just in case. The kid was good, but he lacked street experience. The vehicle he'd pulled over had what appeared to be two male occupants. That time of night, in *that* area, made my gut twitch.

"We were running short-handed at the height of flu season, so out he went, even with his inexperience. My gut told me to roll over to his location, to back him up, regardless. I didn't put it over the air, of course.

"When I rolled up, the kid already had the two subjects jacked up, with their hands atop the trunk lid, one on either side of the vehicle, as he patted them down. Not good, especially the way the two guys were acting, if you know what I mean. I sensed *something* was going on, and my antennae perked up. Those guys were acting just a little *too* calm, I could see them sending each other little visual cues. And the one on *my* side seemed to be edging toward the wheel well. *Oh no you don't...*

"I decided to get out and let the two subjects understand that things had changed in *our* favor. The new kid threw me an irritated glance; his ego was bruised, now that the old man had showed up to hold his hand.

"Sure enough, I snapped on my Streamlight and immediately spotted the gun. The subject on my side of the car had stashed a 4-inch Smith & Wesson Model 66 atop the rear tire, hidden under the wheel well. He was just waiting to grab it when the opportunity presented itself...

"Instantly, I pulled *my* piece, went over, and secured the Model 66. I saw the subjects 'deflate' when they knew their game was up.

"The new kid turned pale when he saw the gun, and he knew instantly that he'd just escaped a bad situation, and that the old man had just saved his ass. But, that was my job, wasn't it?

"Last I heard from the kid, he'd moved to Texas, and was with the Houston Police Department, training their new SWAT team members..." (Author's experience)

> *"Current police agencies can trace their organization back through history to the Praetorian Guard of the Roman Empire. The Praetorian Guard was charged with the protection of the Roman Emperor's life, and with the preservation of public order and morals."*
> *(Taught to NOPD recruits)*

TAKING THE RIDE

"The Orleans Levee Board used to have a police and aircraft firefighter detachment posted at Lakefront Airport. One of their lieutenant's passions was writing traffic citations, but he wasn't allowed off the airport. He was just a little *too* zealous, if you know what I mean, so they kept him on a very short leash. As a matter of fact, the take-home car they gave him was so messed up, he couldn't even get it over the Seabrook Bridge without a long running start! But he kept it clean and waxed, got to give him that.

"One night, this lieutenant had a little problem, so he requested me to roll over and give him a hand. Well, he had pulled over a smartmouth jackass at Lakeshore Drive at Downman Road. The lieutenant had written him EIGHTEEN citations. He really threw the book at him. The more the guy talked and threatened, the more citations the lieutenant wrote. A citation book only has twenty five citations, and each book is signed out to the individual officer, and at times, these books are rationed. The NOPD Print Shop produces them.

"As it turned out, *all* eighteen citations the lieutenant had written were flawed. The driver lied about not having a driver's license, and he gave a bogus name, address, DOB, the works. The lieutenant asked me what he should do.

"I told him the procedure...for *each* of the eighteen citations, he would have to void that citation, submit a Form 40 in triplicate, issue a corrected citation, and so on.

"The lieutenant didn't have enough citations to do all that.

"I laughed.

"The lieutenant just didn't *have* the necessary tickets, and I couldn't just give him any...these are signed out to the individual officer, like I mentioned before.. He knew a *huge* ass chewing was imminent. He would undoubtedly get a suspension and further curtailment of his law enforcement duties. NOPD Ticket Processing bitches all the time about having to deal with voided tickets, but an officer passing on eighteen of them on a *single* stop? There would be *hell* to pay...

"The desperate lieutenant asked me what would *I* do?

"I thought about it a moment, and told him. "It's easy...place him under arrest and take him to Central Lockup. Ticket Processing was therefore *eliminated* with the arrest procedure. And, after all, a citation is in lieu of a physical arrest for an offense, and this guy had earned *eighteen* of them. And he was a mouthy asshole. He *needed* to take the ride.

"So, in the end, I transported the subject after the Lieutenant arrested him, read him his Miranda rights, and handcuffed him. The guy happened to be an attorney, and when he was placed in 'cuffs, he grew livid with rage. He threatened *me*, too. Big time.

"During the ride downtown, the subject grew wilder and wilder, started screaming and banging his head against the door window, and all that nonsense. He called me things that would have made a Chief Petty Officer blush. He *really* got agitated.

"Finally, I pulled the squad car over to the curb, away from traffic. When the subject noticed this, he started screaming "Police brutality!", thinking I was stupid enough to whip his ass. Nope...that's not the way I'm wired.

"I merely told him, "Sir, I've been courteous and respectful. And I am merely transporting you to the lockup. I don't know you, so there is no personal animus from my side involved. And all *you* have done is scream at me, threaten me, insult me and my lineage...anything you can think of, to make things personal and nasty. I know you're an attorney, and that you have friends downtown, so I know this arrest isn't going anywhere."

"My prisoner got very quiet.

"I took a breath, and continued, "I know you will lie about the Lieutenant and myself, and all that. But I want you to know that there is an Olympus L200 microcassette recorder here in my pocket, recording *everything* you say. I switched it on and started recording the moment you were placed under arrest." I actually opened my uniform pocket and showed him the recorder.

'I added, "And remember, there is no reasonable expectation of privacy in the back of a police car, and since I'm privy to this conversation, I'm not abrogating your rights in any way. Now, are you comfortable? Is the air conditioning OK? Do you need any medical attention?"

"The now-docile subject suddenly grew 'respectful'...he told me he was fine and would give me no more trouble.

"At Central Lockup, when I got him out of the car, the guy asked me if the recorder could 'malfunction' or 'go missing', or if the tape might somehow disappear? I just grinned and shook my head.

"When I got back to the Lieutenant with all the paperwork, I told him about the guy getting a little rambunctious, and about capturing it all on tape.

"The lieutenant was grateful, and a few days later, he bought my recorder so he could cover his ass on future traffic issues." (Police Officer)

"Every society gets the kind of criminal it deserves. What is equally true is that every community gets

the kind of law enforcement it insists on."
(From a speech by Robert Kennedy)

EVEN HIS EYES WERE GLAZED

"As a policeman, I was a problem child. Oh, I did my work well enough, but I had a real problem kissing the chickenshit (every department has a few) big bosses' asses and groveling enough to keep them happy. This led to a Byzantine career path, with oddball assignments and yours truly often being 'loaned' to other agencies for extended periods, to keep me from contaminating decent cops who didn't *dare* rock the chief's boat.

"One morning, the chief of my current assignment ordered me to return to Headquarters to report to him, personally, Code 3. Very dramatic, for maximum effect. All this was put slowly and clearly over the air, and repeated, so the 'good cops' would know I would be getting another official enema.

"When I stood tall before the chief, he leered at me through his distinctive haze of stinking cigar smoke. He smoked those cheap, stinky, mule-turd things. The chief curtly ordered me to go get him a couple of glazed donuts from McKenzies, up the street. He opened his wallet, snatched out a crisp twenty dollar bill, and added, "...and make it snappy, Officer!"

"WHAT? He pulled me off a working call, just to go get him a couple of freakin' DONUTS?

"So, smiling, I took his $20 bill, went over to McKenzie's Pastries on Elysian Fields, gleefully went inside, and bought the chief TWENTY DOLLARS worth of glazed donuts! Yes, I paid the tax myself; I wanted to make a point.

"I returned as fast as I could, legally and safely, to his office, with those boxes and boxes of fresh, hot, aromatic McKenzie's donuts. The chief'as eyes grew as large as dinner plates when I brought them into his office. He started coughing and choking. *I loved it.*

"The skinflint bastard...I had blown his entire *week's* food budget on a bunch of donuts. His secretary had a difficult time restraining her hysterical laughter when I strolled into his office. Her assistant wasn't so lucly, she had fled instantly to the supply closet, but we heard her frenzied cackling at this amazing spectacle.

"The chief's angry shouts, threats, and curses warmed my soul for a long time to come..." (Author's experience)

"You know what you get when you assume? Break it down...you make an 'ass' out of 'you' and 'me'. Get it? Never assume, go ahead and check it out. Remember, there isn't anything rarer in this world than common sense."
(Heard at a police in-service training class)

PASCAL SALADINO

"A while back, I was attending a police function with a young patrolman from the Sixth District when I spotted Detective Pascal Saladino, so of course I had to go over and talk with him.

"Talking with Sal is always a treat, and a privilege. Detective Saladino is one of those rare people who is literally 'a legend in his own lifetime.'

"Pascal Saladino retired from the New Orleans Police Department after thirty-three years' service, with twenty-three years just in the Homicide Division! Understand that the average working 'life' of a homicide detective on a major police department is just three years. When Detective Saladino was in N.O.P.D. Homicide, it was the best unit in the entire department, and Saladino was one of the reasons why.

"My young friend never even *heard* of him, which was a severe shock to me. Detective Saladino taught us a course in homicide investigations when I was in the police academy. He was the only speaker people remembered years later. Generations of New Orleans cops have benefited from his wisdom and experience, this wise, philosophical, sincerely religious man...the best detective I've ever known.

"A few years back, I attended an Armed Robbery and Homicide Conference, and Saladino was a featured speaker. As a matter of fact, he had *invited* me there. I attended just because of him. For a week, we listened to experts from all over the United States, including FBI agents. Most of them were good speakers, and gave us valuable information.

"But when Saladino was scheduled to speak, the auditorium was jam packed. When *he* spoke, the people gave him their rapt attention. All those tough robbery and homicide detectives gave him *complete* respect. There was *no* grab-assing when Saladino spoke...the only time I saw that happen during the entire week. Saladino was *awesome*.

"You'd think that a man of Detective Saladino's reputation would be a real ego freak, but you'd be wrong. He is just a sincere, honest, hard-working man with no axe to grind. He is an inspiration and, simply, one of the very finest human beings I've ever had the pleasure to call a friend. Pascal Saladino, simply put, is the exemplification of *the Real Police*, and in my world, there is no higher token of respect." (Author)

"Kill reverence and you've killed the hero in man."
(Ayn Rand)

DED MANN

"When I started in law enforcement, the revolver was still king, and only the platoon commander had a hand-held radio. The pay was low, we received no benefits, and the qualifications were primarily limited to who you knew, or were related to.

"Merit, training, and education, were not even factored in. Consequently, we accumulated a slew of idiots wearing badges, most of whom weren't intellectually or physically capable of graduating from a basic P.O.S.T. Academy.

"One afternoon, we received a complaint about a dead man floating in the Violet Canal. We sent an old time political deputy to handle the report. That was about as basic as it gets. Dead people don't fight, they don't resist, they don't complain, they're just naturally docile and cooperative.

"After a couple of hours, the old deputy returned and threw his 'report' on my desk, for me to review and sign off.

"It was just a face sheet. It was hand written in immense, sprawling letters. The old timer had the date wrong, the wrong location, and he described the incident as a Signal 21. I laughed.

When did a Signal 29 become a Signal 21?

And, according to the report, the victim's last name, was "MANN", and his first name was "DED"...

"I kid you not. I think they eventually promoted him to Colonel or something..." (Detective Sergeant)

"Police work isn't a job...it's a way of life."
(Police Officer)

HOT FOOT

"I heard this 52-F (fire) call come out over the radio, so I went over there, too, since it wasn't far away.

"When I got to the scene, I saw the house with smoke billowing out of its roof and windows. I could see flames, too. The fire department was en route, but they were still minutes away, so I jumped out of the patrol car to check if anyone was still in the house and needed any help. A car was parked in the driveway, so I assumed someone was inside.

"I called out, "Police Officer!" as I banged on the front door, but got no response.

"Neighbors at the scene told me that an old lady lived alone in the house. No one knew where she was, so it appeared that she was still inside the burning house. I was worried that she had been overcome by the smoke and heat, so I got on the radio and told Headquarters what the situation was, and was told to go ahead and make a rescue attempt.

"All of us could hear sirens from the approaching fire department units, but they were still quite a distance off, so I banged on the door again, got no response, and decided to 'John Wayne' the door. I reared back and kicked the front door as hard as I could...just below the doorknob. My foot went through the door easily. *TOO* easily, if you know what I mean...

"Unfortunately, my foot got stuck *in* the door...half my leg was inside the house, and the rest of me was outside. And, the portion of leg and foot inside, was getting burned...there were *flames* on the other side of the door...that's why my foot had gotten through it so easily.

"I started screaming and struggling to get my leg back out of the door, and the frantic neighbors helped pull me out. The David Crockett Fire Department guys rolled up, and they pulled me out, too, and some Gretna Police EMS guys arrived and *they* helped patch me up.

"I had received some severe burns and had to throw away my uniform pants and the shoes I wore. My pants had actually started to *melt* in the intense heat. The old lady was never in the house, she was over in Gretna playing bingo with her friends.

"I guess the joke was on *me* that time..." (Police Officer)

"The David Crockett Steam Fire Company No. 1 is the oldest, continuously active volunteer fire department in America."

THE BONY EXPRESS

"A few years back, before my friend Warren screwed up and was demoted from street cop to sergeant, he was a good cop. Actually, he was exceptionally good. He really got the job done. Meaning, to do his job the best way possible, he developed an intricate network of informants, roughly akin to an intelligence officer developing and maintaining a network of agents.

"Warren built a vast network, and he actually cared for his people. He cultivated, nurtured, and fiercely protected *his* people, who came to trust him. He had an easy going manner, but he was tough as nails when he had to be.

"As you might imagine, these informants were not members of the landed gentry, they were street people. One of them was a skinny young crack whore we called "The Bony Express", because of her extremely rapid handling and massive volume of the tricks she serviced.

"We learned of her from a leaky-mouthed DEA jackass who wanted to plug in to Warren's network to advance *his* career. He didn't give a shit about Warren or his network or anything else but what *he* needed to advance.

"Warren was too wiley to be orchestrated, and he blew off the Fed easily enough. But the hungry, ruthless Fed got jealous, and he set up "The Bony Express" one night, or so we heard, as a means of showing Warren who was boss. He was just a heartless bastard climbing the career ladder and he'd have knifed his own Mother to make points with his bosses. He'd have done his best to burn any one of us, or *all* of us, if it would get him promoted. Well, he went up against the wrong customer, and *he* got burned big-time. Even the Feds were tired of him, and he lost his job.

As for "The Bony Express"...

"She was found dead of a massive overdose, and as too often the case, she wound up in a cheap cardboard box in the wet, muddy potter's field off Gentilly.

"But not for long...

..

"Local legend has it that Warren had "The Bony Express" exhumed, and he paid for a nice casket, and he arranged to have her buried in a decent place with 'decent' people. All at his own expense, and very quietly, though he steadfastly denies this.

"But all of us believe it, because we know Warren, and we know how he operates, and we admire his humanity, and that's good enough for us..." (Police Detective Sergeant)

"The courage we desire and prize is not the courage to die decently, but to live manfully."
(Thomas Carlyle)

I WAS INVISIBLE!

"Once, I got involved in a minor Signal 20 (auto accident). *I* was the victim. It was getting late in the evening, and it was nearly dark. I was in my patrol jeep, which was painted a flat olive drab color. I was in the tactical military police uniform, too, which was O.D. green fatigues. We looked like regular troops except for the black "MP" brassard and the standard black police gun belt. I was driving on Esteban Street in Arabi, near the river.

"Some old man in a white Ford LTD came blasting out of his driveway without even looking behind him. He nailed me hard on my right front fender. When the old man got out of his car and saw me...dressed in that Army uniform with the big .45 automatic, he looked shocked. He demanded an accident report, which was all right with me...I *had* to have one. The jeep was Federal property. Even a minor accident generated a mountain of paperwork.

"The old geezer went inside and phoned the St. Bernard Sheriff's Office. They sent out Ray Millet. I knew Ray...he was an old time deputy and an excellent accident investigator. He took one look at the accident scene and knew *exactly* what had happened. The old man admitted that he never really looked behind himself when he came out of the driveway. He never saw me. But, I had to say something. I told Ray, "I believe the gentleman didn't see me, Ray. After all, I'm dressed in a camouflage uniform, and driving a camouflaged jeep...I was *invisible*!"

"The old man started laughing, but Ray told me to clear the his scene and 'keep my ass out of *his* Parish.' I grinned, saluted him, and left." (Military Police Sergeant)

The tragedy of old age is not that one is old, but that one was young."

(Mark Twain)

THE BOOB JOB

"I remember a murder-for-hire case in New Orleans some time back. A wealthy older fellow had spent a fortune on a young woman, 'enhancing' her appearance so she'd be a truly eye-popping trophy wife worthy of *his* enormous ego.

"He discovered that she was cheating on him, shortly after their society page wedding, and he decided to have her murdered. It would restore his injured pride, and the colossal insurance payout would add to his already-considerable fortune. And he could exploit her death is so many other ways...

"As it turned out, the 'hit man' he eventually hired was an undercover Police Officer, and we were amused when we watched the covert video of the final meeting between the client and the 'assassin', where the fine details of the murder were hammered out.

"The wealthy client wanted to make sure that his wife suffered as horribly as possible, but he also demanded absolute *proof* that her murder was successfully committed. He demanded a series of digital images of the wife's torture and murder, and high-definition video, if possible, of her suffering, humiliation, and death.

"He authorized the 'hit man' to hire an expert videographer to film the video; he said he'd be happy to play extra for it, and he also demanded that the videographer be 'silenced' permanently when his job was done.

"And remember, I'm very wealthy, and I have connections and resources that you're not privy to. Don't even *think* about double-crossing me, or attempting extortion some time in the future."

"He also demanded that physical proof...both of her breast implants, and her *head...* be delivered to him, for his approval. That is when final payment for the 'hit man's services would be paid.

"In the end, the wealthy husband didn't have as many 'connections' as he thought, and his attorneys were happy to relieve him of nearly all his wealth. The videotaped meetings with the 'hit man' were *devastating* to his defense.

"His new wife divorced him in a shower of lurid publicity. She eventually married her boyfriend, they started a family, and the wealthy man died in jail...a massive heart attack, while he was being buggered.

"I really *like* happy endings, and this was almost

Hollywood material. I kinda miss those days..." (Author's experience)

"One of the greatest delusions in the world
is the hope that the evils of this world can be cured
by legislation."
(Thomas B. Reed)

STOCKHOLM SYNDROME

"At one time, I was with the City of Gretna Police Department, and my girlfriend was with the Jefferson Parish Sheriff's Office. She lived in an apartment at 680 Lapalco, on the West Bank, and had endured carpal tunnel surgery on both wrists, simultaneously, due to getting clobbered in a Signal 20 aboard a ferry. Some guy had came in too fast on the slippery deck, lost control, and had slammed into her parked car. I had to do everything for for my girlfriend, including feeding her, giving her baths, dressing her...the works. She had these two immense surgical casts on her forearms.

"We were returning from a routine checkup with her surgeon. As we entered the apartment parking area, we both observed a white male savagely punch a young white female right in the face, with a closed fist. Blood splattered everywhere, and the woman fell back into a wooden fence so hard, it broke.

"To make matters worse, she was holding a screaming infant!

"My girlfriend and I locked eyes...remember, she had both forearms covered in casts, and we were both in plain clothes. "You want a piece of this?" I asked her, and she nodded grimly. I slammed the car to a stop and bounded out, weapon in hand, police badge and ID visible, hanging from my neck chain.

"Yes, I was out of my jurisdiction, but I just didn't give a damn. I grabbed the guy and threw him head down onto the ground. My girlfriend emerged from our vehicle and assisted the bleeding woman and the shrieking baby as best she could.

"The guy I had tackled was inching toward his truck, presumably to arm himself. I didn't give him the chance, I grabbed his ankles, rolled him away from his truck, and then handcuffed him and patted him down for weapons.

"As I'm doing this, some Einstein in a nearby apartment was looking down at our little tableau, yelled that she was calling the cops. I replied, "That is a *great* idea."

"Somehow, the JPSO sprang out of the ground. They were there in *seconds...*

"The victim begged us not to arrest her boyfriend; she loved him and he was her baby daddy. He took the ride anyway, on an array of charges. He had a *long* rap sheet.

"My girl friend and I both signed the arrest paperwork, as co-complainants with the State of Louisiana, and as witnesses, and we both felt good about it. Still do..." (Police Officer)

> *"Our business depends upon people killing each other. Business is good!"*
> *(Homicide Detective)*

STRANGE NOISES

"I got a Signal 21 (complaint) concerning 'strange noises' coming from a man's roof. It was one of those filthy raw winter nights...gusting icy winds, blasting rain, really shitty weather. The kind of night when you have a thousand 62-A's (alarms) back-logged and idiots are calling in for chickenshit fender-bender accident reports. Now, some clown hears noises coming out of his roof, so he calls the police, of course. Maybe Elvis was making a comeback...

"I finally located the address. It wasn't easy. The place was in one of those parts of town where all the house numbers are invisible, and the street signs are missing or rearranged. I got out of my nice, dry, warm, cozy police car and stepped out into the unbelievably raw, *blasting* wind and rain and went up to the complainant's door. Hopefully, it would be NCOA (no complainant on arrival). so I could get back into the relatively comfortable police car.

"But no, the door finally creaked open and this *old* man glared out at me. I remember reading somewhere that the last Civil War soldier died in 1959; but, looking at this guy, I wasn't convinced.

"The old dude looked me over, then yelled at me. "What the hell do ya want?" I *told* that damned woman I couldn't serve on the jury any more!"

"I thought, *"Damn! This old fart calls us in this shitty weather for some looney-tunes bullshit, then forgot that he called us in the first place! He thinks I'm here freezing my ass off at 2 A.M. to give him grief about jury duty. I hate this fucking' job!"*

But I was used to handling crazy people. Hell, I'm crazy myself.

"I put on my Joe Friday 'super cop' face and asked him, "Hey, Mister, did you call the police about noises coming from your roof?" I could almost *see* the wheels turning in his head, then the light bulb finally lit up.

"The old coot looked up at my rain-soaked, slowly-freezing face. "Oh, yes, I *am* hearing funny noises up there. *Strange* noises!"

"Somehow, I believed him, maybe the bats in his belfry were stirred up in the screwball weather. I was already soaked in the brutal weather, so I just wanted to placate the old man and get back in my car and try to warm up a little.

"Okay, Cap, I'll check the roof. Maybe your shingles are coming off in this wind."

"The old man nodded, smiled with a toothless mouth and pointed up at the roof. I went out into the blasting rain and shined my Streamlite up at the roof. Nothing was visible, and the shingles looked OK. I made my way to the other side of the house, and began sweeping the light around, looking for anything unusual, and then I saw her...a little old woman squatted atop the roof, chewing on leaves and glaring at me with immense eyes. She was soaking wet but didn't seem to care at all. I sort of felt uncomfortable in interrupting her Nature interlude, y'know?

"She was as old as the man, probably older. She appeared to be freezing to death in that bitter, blasting wind. She was soaked to the bone. Her clothing was nothing by flying, soaked rags flapping in that wind. The sight of her up there startled the hell out of me. I just couldn't believe it. I felt colder and more miserable than ever. This job *sucked* sometimes.

"I got on the radio pronto, and requested the fire department and EMS...no sense in those overpaid cozy bastards enjoying themselves in dry warmth, when they could be out here in the invigorating weather in the wee hours with yours truly, *earning* their pay for a change.

"We finally got the old lady off the roof safely. She had climbed up a tree that morning and spent the *entire* day on the roof, looking around and chewing leaves. Believe it or not, the old lady came through it all unharmed. One tough old biddy, that one. The toothless old man was *so* delighted when he saw her.

"I was going to call you boys this morning, when she ran off; but I didn't want to bother you. I didn't know she was on the roof. I'm sorry... "

"He was such a good-hearted old man, going senile, and I couldn't help but like him. I thanked God that the old lady wasn't a Signal 29 (death). I'm certain she would have been before too long. It was *cold* out there! I felt like a total asshole for mentally bad-mouthing the old boy. You know, sometimes the bullshit calls turn out to be the best calls of all. Sometimes, I *love* this job... (Police Officer)

> *A real policeman never gets tired, cold, hungry or wet."*
>
> *(Ancient police saying)*

SCHOOL BUS

"I remember working a bad call in Chalmette back in the

late 70s; a school bus struck a child who had just gotten off the bus; the wheels rolled over the child's head.

"The injuries were instantly fatal, but we worked our butts off anyway...what else *could* we do, with all the witnesses and especially the wide-eyed, shrieking kids on the bus looking on?

"We got the child to the Emergency Room when things got worse. MUCH worse. The child's mother, a Registed Nurse, was working there in the E.R. and she recognized her child's clothing as we brought him in, working furiously..." (Author's experience)

"I admire the serene assurance of those who have religious faith. It is wonderful to observe the calm confidence of a Christian with four aces."
(Mark Twain)

HONEST MISTAKE

"It had been a slow night 'down the road,' so we decided to add a little zest to the routine. We had a couple of semi-automatic killer death weapons with us...the ones that make liberals so nervous (laughs). We had an abundance of ammunition, too.

"It was cold and very foggy. Since *nothing* was going on, and it was a clear night, we decided to shoot up an old, abandoned pickup truck. We had discovered the white pickup a few days before, way back there in the boondocks by one of the levees, on an access road. We had already discussed using it for an impromptu target.

"We sneaked over there, along the narrow access road, and found the white pickup in our spotlight. It looked a *little* different, but we thought it was due to the fog. We got out of the unit and pulled out our automatic rifles. Both of them were .223 caliber, what the military calls '5.56 mm.' We had already loaded several 30-round magazines, so we just slapped in the magzines, chambered rounds, and 'opened up' on the pickup truck.

"Man, it was *great*! We shot that sucker *full* of holes. We put in over a hundred rounds apiece. We shot out the windshield, the side and back windows, the mirrors, the lights, the tires. We just shot it to bits.

"Finally, it got *really* quiet. We were out of ammo. We started laughing, feeling very satisfied, then tossed the hot guns into the trunk of the patrol car to cool off. And, like giggling fools, we drove up the access road to turn around and get back to the main road, so we could return to patrol.

"We had to drive up another fifty yards or so, to turn around. Then, to our horror...we saw the *real* pickup truck...,the one we had intended to shoot up! *We'd shot up the wrong pickup truck!* An honest mistake. We damned near had heart attacks, both of us! What kind of crazy coincidence...

"We raced back to the shot-up truck, hearts in our throats, looked for bloody bodies inside the truck. Thank God, no one was inside. The truck we'd shot up was the same make, model, and color as the one we intended to blast; but, it was a couple of years newer.

"I told my partner, "Amigo, I'm not saying *shit* about this to anyone. Let's get the hell out of here!"

"We did, too. For the remainder of the shift, we stayed as far from that area as possible. No one ever reported the shot up truck. We discreetly went back a few days later to check out the scene...in the daylight. The murdered truck was gone!

"We never found out why that truck was back there that night...and, thankfully, no one made any 'missing person' report, which was fine with us..." (Name withheld by request)

Once the bullet leaves the barrel, you can't call it back."

(Special Agent Samuel Wayne Lee)

BOOM BOOM HURT

"In 1977 I was recruited by the St. Bernard Sheriff's Office as a Deputy Sheriff/Emergency Medical Technician, and within a week of hire, was appointed Unit Training Officer and soon afterward, Night Shift Supervisor for the EMS Division. It was my first job in law enforcement. We stayed busy.

"One night, my partner "Boom Boom" and I responded to an EMS call for service, an overdose in Village Square. A young man, and he was in bad shape. We ignored all the dope and paraphernalia scattered about in plain sight. We stabilized him and transported him to the Emergency Room at Chalmette General Hospital.

"Everything was routine; I was writing up the Incident Report, and a few feet away, "Boom Boom" was assisting the E.R. physician and two nurses as they treated the our overdose patient.

"All of a sudden, all Hell broke loose.

"Shouting and struggling, the patient went berserk and started punching, kicking, clawing, and screaming. One nurse turned away, her uniform ripped to the waist, and the doctor fell backwards onto the floor, his eyeglasses broken, and blood streaming down his face. Then the patient jumped up, atop the treatment table, and kicked "Boom Boom" right in the eye. "Boom Boom" fell back, blood pouring from his eye.

"Now, all this occurred in a very short period, and I wasted no time in getting to the berserker. He tried to kick me, but I side-stepped the kick and punched him, hard as I could, in the nuts, which toppled him backwards off the table. He was stunned for just a moment, but I was already there; I snatched him up and slammed him back atop the treatment table. Adrenalin had kicked in.

"I was still struggling to control the subject, and had my hands full. Suddenly, I felt a burning, stinging sensation in my back, and instantly reacted: my right elbow instinctively went back, full force, popping my attacker in the face, and I heard a thump as the person who had stabbed me hit the floor. I had knocked my attacker cold.

"I discovered later that it was the patient's Mother. Too bad, but that was that. She'd stabbed me with a pair of medical scissors she'd snatched off a table as she ran into the treatment room.

"Pandemonium reigned.

"My right arm started going 'mushy' as I struggled with the guy, and I finally controlled him with my left hand wrapped around his throat. Hard. I kept the pressure on, hard as I could, until he stopped struggling. My hand would be stiff and sore for days.

"The doctor had gotten up and quietly informed me that I was killing his patient. I know I was, this wasn't my first time at bat in the big league.

"When the patient was fully unconscious, I rolled him over and handcuffed him, remembering to double-lock the cuffs.

"A nurse timidly approached me and asked if she could look after my prisoner, and I nodded yes. A sudden flurry of excitement as a group of nurses, technicians, and other folks suddenly crowded into the Treatment Area, tending to "Boom Boom", the doctor, the nurse with the ripped uniform (she was also badly scratched), and the woman I had knocked out.

"No one bothered to remove the scissors protruding from my back; but it was no big deal. My Tuffy Jacket was absorbing most of the blood, and the scissors had gone in at a bad angle, mostly sliding along my backbone and not penetrating very far. I felt no pain, but I didn't like that mushy feeling in my right shoulder and arm.

"I called my Captain at home, to apprise him of the situation, and then I called Communications, to have them change the signal from a 24 to a 24 with a 10-15.

"Chalmette General refused to have anything further to do with the combative patient; they stabilized him and we...my Captain and I...transported him to Charity Hospital downtown, and in the morning, we booked him into the St. Bernard Jail.

"Boom Boom" took the next few days off, until he could see with his injured eye after the swelling went down. His bruises were visible nearly a month later.

"Momma and her dear son threatened me with death and a huge lawsuit, the usual routine in St. Bernard (*and just about everywhere else*). The lawsuit never materialized, and I'm still breathing..." (Author's experience)

"Look at that fuckin' idiot...a '30' (homicide)
looking for a scene..."
(Detective)

RACISTS!

"So, at morning roll call, my watch commander informed me that I'd be on special assignment for the Chief, and to just relax and get some coffee until he came in at 0800. I got some fruit juice instead, and tidied up my usual paperwork.

"At 0800, the Chief rolled in, spotted me, and indicated that he would see me, first thing. He asked me to go into his office and make myself comfortable while he got something. I did so.

"The Chief came in moments later with some paperwork, closed and locked the door and took his seat. He had this air of secrecy I found both amusing and intriguing.

"He started right off, "James, I've got a problem, and I need your help. It might cause you some problems down the line, and it might cost you your job. Can you help me?"

"I just nodded and grinned. Whatever it was, it sounded like fun.

"Okay...you know Latoya, right?" "Of course." She was our administrative honcho...not a sworn officer, but she was in charge of all the office staff, the dispatchers, petty cash, office supplies, you name it. She was, basically, the backbone of our department.

"I've got some information here about her that I find 'disturbing', to say the least. For one thing, I don't think she's employed here under her real name. I think she lied about a lot of things on her employment application, and violated several State laws. And, I understand she's running around impersonating a sworn officer. Can you look into this for me...discreetly?"

"Of course, Chief. I'll go straight to R& I (Records and Identification) and see what I can dig up on her."

"Fine, take my car, And do it fast, and please keep it quiet, She has ears everywhere."

"I went straight to 715 South Broad (NOPD Headquarters) and went up to R&I on the Second Floor, signed in for a data inquiry, and, in a very short time, I was looking at a computer printout of Latoya's criminal history. It went back for nearly twenty years!

"As I perused it, the technician advised me that I could get additional information over at the Jefferson Parish Sheriff's Office Identification & Records Division at their West Bank location. "I can phone 'em and tell 'em you're on your way, if you want." she added sweetly. I nodded, "Yes, please, I'm going right over", and thanked her sincerely. This was going to be an interesting day.

"I used the Mississippi River Bridge, and at the toll booth, I flashed my badge and ID, signed the bridge toll exemption form, and went straight to the JPSO identification unit. They were not only expecting me, they had already compiled a lengthy portfolio of what I needed, including half a dozen booking photos going back for many years. I was thrilled. I thanked them all profusely and sincerely, passed out my business cards, and promised them my support if any of them ever got into a jam in New Orleans. And then I went back to see the Chief...

"When I reported back to the Chief, he glanced down at his wristwatch, and frowned. "Couldn't find anything, eh? " I just smiled and handed him the bulging manila folder. His eyes grew wide.

"He took a quick look, and whistled. "You struck gold, Sarge! GOLD! Let's go to lunch, and it's on me. Whatever you want, wherever you want. And *this* (he patted the folder), is going with us.

"I just asked for a fast burger down the street, and he agreed. I wasn't going to take advantage of his generosity, but I guess he knew that. As we ate, he looked through the folder, completely amazed. "Look at this...she's a *convicted felon!* She's used over a dozen aliases! Look at all these arrests...this is *incredible!* Theft, battery on the police, false personation, bad checks...it just goes on and on. This is unbelivable!"

"As I munched my burger, he continued, assuring me that he would see to it that her employment was terminated, and so on. He warned me again that all this could bounce back in our laps, and that Latoya had many friends, some of them highly placed in the establishment. I wasn't worried about my job...after all, i was used to being expendable...

"The Chief gave me the rest of the day off, and I used it wisely. In time, Latoya was indeed terminated, but we knew the vagaries of the civil service system, and we suspected that she'd return. I returned to my more normal duties, and things slowly returned to normal.

"A few months later, Latoya surfaced again, with her attorney, and the Chief and I had to appear before the civil service board. Apparently, or so we were informed, poor Latoya was the victim of white racists...the Chief and myself...who invented 'false charges' against her because of our prejudices, etc.

"True, she was a convicted felon, true, she had lied numerous times on her employment application, yes, she stole money, yes, she illegally impersonated a peace officer, all that, and much more, was all true. Granted. But none of it mattered...because *we* were racists!

"In the end, Latoya got her job back, with back pay, and received a promotion, too. The Chief, seeing the handwriting on the wall, quietly retired, and returned to school administration, and I was working undercover at another assignment, so I couldn't have cared less. Those clowns can believe whatever they want, but I know better.

"When my undercover assignment was eventually completed, I turned in *my* papers, too. You can fight city hall...but you can never win." (Detective Sergeant)

"No one hates a bad cop more than a good cop."
(Police axiom)

ARMED ROBBERY

"About a year after the 1981 Joyce Hornady airplane crash in Lake Pontchartrain, a wide-eyed guy oozed into our office one afternoon, lugging a dripping Schwegmann's grocery bag. Inside the bag was an aluminum-foil wrapped oblong bundle containing most of a human arm.

"The guy was a weekend fisherman. He had fished the arm out of the Lake shortly after the Hornady crash. He had taken it home as a "souvenir."

"He had wrapped the arm carefully in aluminum foil and stashed it in the back of the family's food freezer! His wife had just found it while looking for something for dinner, she freaked, and, to make a long story short, she demanded that he turn it in 'lickety split'.

"Besides, they might give you some cash money! Someone might be offering a reward for it."

"As you can imagine, in a short time, we had a gaggle of grinning dicks and uniformed guys listening to this zany little story. It broke up when our Sergeant thundered in and ordered me to submit a report, to take the arm to the Morgue over on South White Street...a short walk...and to book the asshole for "Armed Robbery"...

"The fisherman turned pale and nearly crapped his pants...

'Thank God, the Sarge was grinning about the latter..." (Homicide Detective)

The first recorded instance of an autopsy in connection with a murder investigation occurred in Maryland in 1655 (FBI)

THE HEADBOARD HUMPER

"The first policeman I ever saw lugging a cellular telephone around was yours truly. I had bought mine from a Radio Shack on Commercial Drive in Arabi back in the 80s, and it was one of those huge 'transportable' units with a handset, cord, and a large box with the telephone's electroniccs and a huge lead-acid battery. This monster weighed around fifteen pounds, and I had equipped mine with a magnetic mobile antenna, and kept it plugged in to my car's power system. It put out something like 1.5 watts of transmitter power, and it worked extremely well. It had to...it had cost me around $1500, and the service charge was $51.50 a month through Electrocom in New Orleans. Don't even *ask* me about the truly insane roaming charges in those days...

"The telephone allowed me a total new sense of freedom. When I was 'on call', I was no longer tied to my home landline telephone, I could be anywhere in the City. And I even carried regular telephone directories in my car...both the white pages *and* the yellow pages!

"So, with the new phone, and certain other gadgets, I just about lived in my car round the clock. I even carried spare clothes, shaving gear, just about all the comforts of home.

"One evening, I received an urgent phone call from one of my police colleagues. He was in a bad jam and needed to see me, urgently, out at an address on Chef Menteur Highway, in New

Orleans East. He begged me to make certain that I had my medical trauma kit, and asked me to get to his location as fast as I could, but to be quiet about it. At that point, I *knew* it was some nefarious bullshit. He had a reputation for getting himself embroiled in outrageous tomfoolery. And, from the address he had given me, I knew it would be some kind of truly silly nonsense.

"It was...

"When I arrived, I spotted him as he yanked open the door and, looking around furtively, he put his finger to his lips, signalling me to be quiet. I grinned and shook my head.

"This was one of those cheap, run-down motels, where folks went to do things they didn't want their friends to catch them doing, if you catch my drift. My buddy...let's call him "Myron"...looked both excited, and scared to death. I knew that this was going to be a interesting caper...

"When I got into the room, I saw that "Myron" was disheveled, and he was wearing nothing but a T-shirt and some briefs. He was *extremely* agitated.

"Then I spotted the dead, naked woman stretched across the bed, with blood and other signs of distress apparent. The room appeared to be wrecked. Even the bed's cheap headboard was lying on the floor...

"Then, to my astonishment, the 'dead woman' uttered a few groans, and feebly attempted to move. I was *so* relieved.

"Upon checking the woman thoroughly, I saw that she was in her thirties, and that she had a broken nose, some loosened front teeth, her lips were bruised, lacerated, and badly swollen, and various other odds and ends. She also had a large contusion on her forehead.

"I knew Myron thought of himself as a kind of Don Juan,

but I never saw him as a disciple of the Marquis de Sade, too. But the woman's condition was obviously not self-inflicted.

"As he got dressed, Myron started filling me in on the details, and he kept begging me to patch her up and get her out of the motel room and to bring her home. I knew Myron was married, and I knew this girl *wasn't* his wife. Poor bastard.

"Now, understand that Myron was a short, balding, chubby little black guy with an *enormous* ego. He actually *did* see himself as God's gift to women. And, he tended to speak of himself in the third person, and his favorite name for himself was *"The Bone"*...

"I was openly laughing at the predicament *The Bone* had gotten himself into, and he started to get a trifle nasty, whereupon I reminded him that I was there to help him, and that I would go home if he gave me any shit. He could just fix his problems all by himself. He calmed down immediately.

"He gave me the sordid details of their tryst...how he had met the woman at another location, they had a bite to eat, and then they drove to this motel, he signed them in, and they went to the room and immediately began a hot sexual rendesvous.

"Apparently, he and the woman were adding new chapters to the Kama Sutra, and both of them were wild with lust for each other. Things got *really* hot and heavy, to say the least...

"At one point, Myron had positioned the woman against the head of the bed, and they began 'doing the deed' doggy style, which the woman found particularly exciting and pleasurable. Myron got into it, too, big time. She grew more and more heated, and urged Myron to give it to her 'harder', deeper', etc. Myron did his best to comply.

"He slightly re-positioned himself to give her *The Bone,* and he even took hold of the headboard as he began thrusting wildly, encouraged by her passionate cries.

"Then, things started to go wrong...

"During a particularly deep thrust, Myron had begun to orgasm, as did the woman. The headboard broke off the wall and slammed the woman directly in the face, knocking her unconscious, breaking her nose, and inflicting other damage. Myron also fell off the bed, hurting *The Bone* and twisting his back. The slippery, unconscious woman had *also* tumbled off the bed, too, knocking over some furniture and further injuring herself as she slammed her head on the floor. *The Bone* was out of breath, covered in sweat, a little drunk, and in deep, deep shit...

"As I'm patching the woman up, Myron is telling me all this, complete with exaggerated facial expressions and body movements, and providing weird sound effects, and he got pretty carried away. I'm trying to keep a straight face, but *no way* was that possible...I have tears coursing down my cheeks...

'Finally, I got her patched up reasonably well, and Myron agreed to take her to the E.R. at Methodist and explain to them that he had picked her up hitching a ride on Chef Highway after she was in a traffic accident.

"I wonder if he ever admitted to them...and his brother...that she was his *sister-in-law*?" (Author's experience)

"If a job is worth doing, it's worth doing right."
(Sulivan J.R. Prine)

MERRY CHRISTMAS

"Many years ago, while I was working alone as a patrolman in New Orleans, I was dispatched to handle a "107" out on Lakeshore Drive near Canal Boulevard. A 107 is the code for a suspicious person, and so I rolled over there on a Code 1, no lights or siren, and obeying all the standard rules of the road.

"It was just after four in the morning, and we were experiencing a bitterly cold night. The heater in my police unit didn't work (as usual, of course, had it been August, it could have burned my legs off)), but I was wearing my jacket, scarf, gloves, long underwear, body armor, two pairs of socks, and a watch cap, and I was *still* shivering. The squad car rocked occasionally as wind gusts blasting off the Lake buffeted the vehicle.

"I arrived in the area and informed the Dispatcher that I was in the area and was looking for the subject. I found him, out there in the darkness, the hard way...I nearly drove over him! He was lying out in the middle of the street, completely naked and appeared to be unresponsive.

"I immediately went 10-97 on the radio and also put out a Code 4 as I stopped my vehicle and snapped on the bright white takedown lights, and the red and blue overhead strobes. I also applied the parking brake, just in case.

"I left the engine running, of course, to keep the juice up and the engine warm.

"Lakeshore Drive was soaked, with tremendous waves crashing over the seawall. It made me feel even colder. No one else was visible in the vicinity, so I gritted my teeth and got out of my relatively warm unit to check on the naked man.

"He was a white male in his early 20s, not wearing a stitch, and he appeared to be unconscious but uninjured. His breath smelled like a distillery. Although I had put out a Code 4, I knew my rank would be cruising by, to check on me anyway. She was good about that. Damn, but it was cold! Mist off the Lake covered my face, and it smelled like an open sewer.

"I popped open the trunk of the squad car and retrieved the grimy blanket. I remembered that I had one when I had checked out the vehicle at the beginning of the 12-hour shift, that I had one...most units didn't... and I was grateful to have it, and a stocked first aid kit, road flares, a fire extinguisher, and other goodies.

"I wrapped the fellow in the blanket and dragged him out of the roadway, to a safer spot. He didn't make a sound, and even all the jostling didn't faze him one bit. His vital signs were OK, but this wasn't the place, or the time, for a thorough examination. I saw headlights approaching and then blue and red police strobes popped on from the approaching unit, and, sure enough, my Sergeant rolled up, got out of the unit…a sudden blast of icy air slammed her door shut, and I heard the muttered *"Shit!"* as she approached me. I grinned.

"She eyeballed the unconscious man, curled her lip, and then glared at me. Her glare was colder than the frigid wind. "What is this bullshit, Prine, are you two going to have a party out here in this crap?" It was hard to hear her, with all the racket from the wind, the units' engines roaring, and the tremendous waves crashing into the seawall.

"I shrugged, laughed, and told her the situation as best I knew it.

"So, what are you going to *do?* Give him a summons?" I shrugged again and shook my head. I had to tell her something *right now*. Now that I had made contact with the guy, I had to deal with him…he had become *my* responsibility, *my* problem. I couldn't just ignore him, or dump him on anyone else, in the condition he was in. And tonight, we only had three units on the road, so I couldn't just drive around with the guy. I made up my mind on the spot as my Sergeant stood there, hugging herself and stomping her feet.

"I'm going to 10-15 his ass as a John Doe, and take him to

Charity for a medical check before I roll him over to Central Lockup." She grinned, relieved that I was going to actually do something, and knowing she'd be getting rid of me very soon. "OK. That sounds good. Let me help you get him in the car, and I'll sign your paperwork before I cut you loose." She was freezing. Poor baby.

"We lugged the guy to my unit, opened the rear door, and carefully stuffed him inside. The drunk bastard was dead weight, and he was still passed out. I arranged him on the seat, and wrapped the blanket around him as best I could. I made sure to cover his head, too, so people at traffic lights wouldn't freak at me transporting a 'corpse' through New Orleans in the early morning hours, and I also made sure to keep him on his side, so that if he started vomiting, he wouldn't drown himself.

"I quickly wrote up a municipal affidavit for the arrest, my Sergeant came over, checked it over, signed it, grinned, flipped me off, and scurried back to her car…it *had* a working heater.

"I returned to my unit, buttoned up, and deeply appreciated being out of the icy wet windblast. I gathered all the paperwork in my clipboard, made the proper entries on my activity sheet, informed the Dispatcher than I was transporting a 10-15 to Charity for a medical check, and made sure to radio in my starting mileage, and jot down the time from the Dispatcher. I also double-checked the item number, and, satisfied for the moment, tossed my clipboard back on the seat, glanced back at the drunk, and proceeded to Charity.

"I asked the Dispatcher to phone Charity for some assistance when I got there, I'd have to use the ambulance ramp, because of the unique circumstances, and in a few minutes, the Dispatcher informed me that they'd be standing by with a gurney at the ramp.

"Well, everything went well at Charity; they checked my prisoner over swiftly, and gave me the OK to remove him to Central Lockup. I made sure I got all that on paper, of course. I repeated the mileage to my Dispatcher as I left Charity enroute to CLU, and noted everything carefully on my activity sheet.

"They glared at me at Central Lockup, but I had expected that, and after a lot of bullshit from their intake people, they accepted the Charity paperwork, my arrest paperwork, and all that; I got everything together, made copies, and finally, my naked drunk was safely behind bars, with trained people watching over him, as I returned to the invigorating weather. It was Christmas Eve...

"The remainder of that shift was relatively quiet. Thank goodness.

"I had volunteered to work Christmas Day swapping for a young guy with kids, and, as usual, people started calling in family fights, injuries, traffic crashes, and all that. Fairly routine stuff.

"Later that afternoon, Headquarters had me return to the station to receive an angry telephone call from the brother of the naked guy I had arrested on Christmas Eve. He was hopping mad, and angrily informed me that he was going to come right over and kick my ass, etc. I listened to all this quietly.

"Finally, as the guy took a few breaths, I asked the guy how his brother was doing, and I asked for his name. The man on the phone was incredulous. He couldn't believe that I was so stupid, that I had arrested a poor helpless youngster, and didn't even bother to learn his name!

"I told him that I had no way of knowing his brother's name...that when I got to him, his brother was naked, unconscious, and unresponsive, out in the middle of Lakeshore Drive at four in the morning. Obviously, he had no identification, and he couldn't answer any questions.

"As I began to fill in the details, the man on the phone changed his attitude. I advised him that if he needed to kick anyone's ass, he should go after the guy or guys who had gotten his brother *passed out drunk*, and then had stripped him naked and dumped him out in the street, on Christmas Eve.

"Eventually, the man on the phone asked me, "So, what you did for my brother was actually to *save* him, not harass him?" "Of course, sir. What if someone, possibly a drunk, had run over your helpless brother out in the street, and killed him? And remember, someone had called it in, I wasn't out there looking for people to harass. Are you crazy? It was COLD out there!"

"The brother on the telephone suddenly burst out laughing, and admitted that he was in the wrong. *This time*. But he didn't like cops, but I might be one of the rare good ones.

"Before he rang off, the mollified man wished me a Merry Christmas.

"Merry Christmas to *you*, your brother, and your family, Sir. And I wish you all a Happy New Year! I meant it, of course." (Author's experience)

The New Orleans Police Department operates a special unit called the 'Crisis Transportation Service.' This organization, in operation since 1983, is the only one of its type in the nation. Highly trained citizen volunteers work a specially marked NOPD transport unit, and respond only to violent mental cases, attempted suicides, and assist individuals suffering from emotional problems.

"YA GOTS ME WRONG, CAP!"

"I tells you, your worship, dat I wasn't *stealin'* dat shit. Dat old bastid wuz deader 'n Jack Shit, so I lets myselves inta his crib and estabarished *salvage rights* to alls dat stuff. It's all legit 'n legal, swear to Allah.

"Dead folks aint's gots no rights to own *nuthin'*, so I wuz all legal. He wuz an inferdil, too, which means I can takes whatevers I wants. Dats straight up Koranical law. I studies dat shit, y'know?

"I usta watch dat Judge Judy on da tube while I wuz incorporated in da Parish Prison, 'n I gots me a G.O.D. paper from dat school dey's runs for da inmates. It be's equivabent to a laws degree, swear to Allah.

"You gots to lemme go, I gots da legal rights. *Ya gots me wrong, Cap!"* (Author's experience)

"I know where I got my shoes, pal; and, if you don't quit pestering me, they'll be pulling 'em out of your skinny ass at Charity Hospital." (Overheard on Decatur Street one night)

THE WALTHER

"One of the reasons I joined law enforcement was so that I could work with other crazies just like me. I used to buy, trade, and sell firearms and other police impedimenta. I had a little blue-steel, German-made Walther PPK/S .380 that I wanted to sell or swap, so I put the word out. These little guns are highly sought after, and I knew I'd have an easy time selling it.

"One of my police colleagues, a former Marine, indicated that he was eager to buy it. He was a James Bond freak and had a real hard-on for the sleek little pistol. He practically drooled when he discussed it. He wanted it very badly.

"We met at his station assignment, out in the parking lot, late that night. He asked eagerly if he could fire it, to make sure it worked properly. I agreed.

"Like a true moron, I showed him how to insert the magazine, chamber a round, work the safety, the whole drill. It is, after all, a very simple little gun.

"He finally grabbed the Walther and rapid-fired it...right there in the parking lot. *That* instantly activated all of the local dogs into extended barking fits. Well...yes, it operated perfectly, but I already knew that. If it had been a bad gun, I'd have fixed it, but would never have offered it for sale until it was perfectly reliable. Code of ethics, and all that.

The Marine fired the Walther's magazine dry; and, grinning, he handed over the cash. We shook hands. His were trembling. He had it...bad. I grinned...the Walther had found a new home, and I had some extra money for other interesting projects.

"When the Sun came up, the little former Marine discovered, to his horror, that he had shot his ride several times. The little bullets had bounced off the hard-surfaced parking lot and peppered his wife's car. It leaked out coolant and oil as it died... Luckily, no one else's car wa damaged..." (Police Officer)

Smokeless gunpowder was invented in 1884.

HOT WOMAN

"Late one evening, just before shift change, we were dispatched to investigate a 'suspicious fire' near Chef Menteur Highway at Paris Road. We located it easily enough; it was back a ways from the hard surface roadway, but easy to get to, and besides, the light was beginning to fade, and the fire was easy to spot there in the gloom.

"It was a woman's body set afire. She had been stripped naked, her throat had been cut so deeply that she had been nearly decapitated, and someone had rammed a ragged two by four into her vagina before dousing her with gasoline and setting her afire. We saw that her fingers and hands had been pretty much destroyed, too.

"My partner, just out of the Academy, started screaming and carrying on; he thought the woman was his wife. They shared the same features and figure. He had to take a few days off..." (Author's experience)

First execution by electric chair: William Kemmler, murderer, on August 6th, 1890.

DOMESTIC VIOLENCE

"My partner Dianna and I got a 21 (complaint) about 'unknown trouble' which probably meant it was a bullshit call. We rolled to the address they'd given us, got out of the patrol car and went up to the front door. Discreetly, of course, we were in a nice, quiet neighborhood. We could *feel* eyes on us, though, and there were probably camcorders recording our every move.

"The house was a two-story, well-maintained, and the lawn was perfect. I *almost* pressed the doorbell button, but never got the chance...the door opened instantly, like an automatic opener operated it. A matronly-looking woman was there, smiling primly, but with that *look* in her eyes. You know, she's glad to see you, but she wishes she didn't *have* to see you at all. I guess a lot of dentists get that look...

"The lady asked us in, wringing her hands. Dianna stepped in, and so did I. It was a *real* house...a *real* family lived there. It smelled cozy, and, homey. I could smell dinner cooking somewhere in back of the house. It smelled wonderful. I remember getting a little nostalgia attack, as a matter of fact. I live in a fuckin' dump, but after my second divorce, I don't care much where I live. But, this place was really nice.

"The lady started talking to Dianna. They developed an instant rapport, but then, that was one of Dianna's gifts. She said quietly, "It's my son-in-law. He comes home every day and beats up my little girl. *Every day! He's a beast!"*

"She glanced up, then whispered, "He's up there right now abusing her! You ought to hear them. He throws her against the walls. She cries out, and I can hear him laughing...then he beats her some more."

"By this time the lady was crying.

"Dianna's face transformed into what I call her 'ass kicking' face. Dianna asked, "Ma'am, how old is your daughter?"

'The lady replied, "My sweet baby is only twenty-four. She got married to that... *man* just two weeks ago, and they live here with me." The lady started crying softly.

"I asked, "Ma'am, why hasn't she called us herself? Do you

think he's threatening her? Did she tell you she needs help? Have you seen any bruises on her?"

"The lady shook her head. "No. No. I asked her if she wanted a doctor, but she absolutely refused. She told me she didn't need a physician, but I know she was lying to spare my feelings. She is so innocent and loving."

"The lady looked at both of us. She was desperate. "Please, Officers, just go up there and *listen* to them. *Please* put a stop to it! I can't take much more of this stress. I'm losing my mind. I'm losing my religion...I'm a good Catholic. I attend Mass every day! And, I've seen on television what happens when a man abuses his wife like this." The lady daubed at her eyes with a tissue.

"Dianna and I looked at each other, and nodded.

"We'll help your daughter, ma'am. You lead the way, please."

"The lady nodded, ashamed, but also relieved somewhat that we were going to take care of the issue. and she led us up the stairs.

"We stopped in the softly lighted hallway, almost ankle deep in the plush carpeting. We could hear them struggling...thumps, moans, slaps, harsh laughs, and weird sounds we couldn't recognize. The guy must have really been slapping the girl around. Dianna's eyes got wide. I guess mine did, too.

"Dianna yelled, "POLICE!" as she yanked open the door and rushed into the room. I was right behind her...

"Well, I guess *abusing* her was a poor choice of words. The young couple was locked atop the bed in a frenzied lovemaking clench, doggy-style. A camcorder mounted on a tripod was recording their action. I don't know who was more surprised...the frisky couple on the bed, us, or Momma standing out in the hallway, looking in with *huge* eyes...

"As you can imagine, we left fast and discreetly, apologizing profusely, but trying desperately to hide our grins..." (Police Officer)

"Sex is an emotion in motion."
(Mae West)

PROM DATE

"The youngster was spoiled, petulant, and not overly bright. He had wanted to borrow the family car to take his girlfriend to her high school prom, but Mama had refused. The kid didn't even possess a driver's license...mostly, all he possessed was an attitude. This was in the Fifth District, right next to the Desire Projects. A real shithole.

"So the kid devised a plan...he would make his Mama feel sorry for him just before the prom, so she'd change her mind and allow him to use the car after all. He planned to injure himself, in a fake fit of despondency...just a minor wound, one that wouldn't really hurt him or anything, and with the bonus of getting his girlfriend all worried about him, too.

"He and two trusted friends decided that a 'suicide' would be perfect. They snatched a .22 rifle, and went to an unused place on Alvar Street to do the deed. No interference, no witnesses, no problems!

"They planned well...one of them had even stolen a beer, as an effective tranquilizer, and a small towel, in case any blood leaked out. They sat around, eager to get it done and over with, planning on how to do it, drinking the beer, and just having a wonderful time.

"Finally, the beer was gone, and the moment of truth arrived. The 'suicide' made sure the rifle was loaded, and that the safety was off. He expected a little sharp pain, but nothing he couldn't handle. He was just going to shoot a little grazing wound in his shoulder...nothing deep, just enough to look impressive and get Mama's pity and sorrow. Plus, it would boost his standing with his friends, that he was truly a tough guy. No way could he lose on this gimmick!

"The kid had carefully placed the rifle's muzzle against his shoulder, and experimented as to exact placement and angle. Finally, satisfied that it was all perfect, he nodded to his friends, who had found a piece of rusted-out metal pipe in the house, he would use it to depress the trigger and fire the rifle. The boys had looked on, thrilled with the adventure, and happy to be a part of it.

"The friend handed the pipe to the 'suicide', and had even helped him position it carefully on the trigger. All set!

"The considerate youth had waited patiently as friends had shoved their fingers into their ears...their idea of 'hearing protection', and the kid then took a deep breath, gritted his teeth, and fired the rifle into his shoulder.

"POP!

"Then, the kid made one loud scream as bright red blood started gushing from his nose and mouth. He had dropped the rifle as he fell to the floor, gasping for breath. He was dead in seconds...

"Apparently, he had 'anticipated' the pain of the gunshot, and had tensed up a bit, possibly moving rifle's muzzle slightly.

The little bullet had zoomed in, torn through the shoulder muscle, struck hard bone, and this deflected the bullet enough so that it ripped through his chest, ripping his aorta, and creating extensive damage to various organs until it ended up in his kidney. Yes, a kid's little .22 did all that.

"The boys immediately jumped on their buddy, trying desperatrely to do something, *anything*, to revive him, but nothing they could have done, would have helped.

"One of them finally ran to the boy's Mama, and told her, between sobs, what had happened, and she had run immediately to the scene...not too far away. and she was still there, wailing and crying hysterically, cradling her son, when we arrived. The boys gave us the story, and the physical evidence filled in the rest.

"By the way, the kid's funeral took place on the same day as his girlfriend's school prom..." (Police Officer)

NOPD Officers were prohibited from carrying firearms until 1899.

CECIL

"Cecil" was one of those people with the body of a 26 year old man, but the mental capacity of a six year old child. He idolized the police and did his best to emulate us. He always wore a raggedy POLICE T-shirt and equipped himself with assorted kid's police toys, including a pair of little plastic handcuffs, a toy billy club, a little plastic revolver, and a genuine Acme Thunderer nickel-plated whistle (made in England), that I had bought for him when I was in a light-hearted mood. When I presented it to him and 'swore him in', he was ecstatic. He'd MADE IT! He was *finally* one of us...

"When he saw us rolling by, he would explode in a happy frenzy, shouting and laughing and jumping around and blasting us with his genuine *official* police whistle. He was like a one-man Mardi Gras. To tell the truth, I sort of envied Cecil. His world was so much simpler and nobler than mine. I needed Cecil's world much more than he needed mine...

"Now, the locals knew Cecil and usually played along with his whimsy when he 'frisked' them or chased them down with his revolver or police club, smiling and laughing and having the time of his life.

"One evening, it all ended.

"Cecil" apparently met up with someone who didn't know him, or who took him a little too seriously.

"Cecil" was already dead when we got to him, lying there on the sidewalk in a spreading pool of blood, his toy revolver in his hand, his beloved Acme Thunderer genuine *official* whistle clenched in his teeth, and six fresh bullet holes in his belly, chest, and face... (Author's experience)

"The Policeman is the little boy who grew up and became what he said he was going to be."

(Anonymous)

THE MAD CRAPPER

"We got a lot of oddball calls when I was in the Crime Scene Unit, too. Most of them were based on the simple fact that far too many people watched idiotic crime movies and television and got stupid ideas. This included Police Officers, especially rookies. And this was long before the CSI shows.

"One evening, I was dispatched to a residential burglary in Lakeview to secure some fresh evidence. When I went 10-97, I learned that the 'fresh evidence' was, in fact, a large human turd sitting proudly atop the center of the dining room table. The thing was still steaming, too, damn it. I wondered how *that* would look on prime-time television?

"We occasionally had freaks who would not only burgle your home, but would leave a personal calling card, as a little lagniappe, for their victims. Sometimes it was graffiti, and other times...

"The young Patrolman handling the scene excitedly told me that he hadn't touched the turd, and he'd made sure no one else handled it, either. He wanted it absolutely clean, for fingerprints and crime scene photos and all. Wow...how considerate. How professional! I instantly realized that I was dealing with a future Superintendent.

"Looking at the turd, I asked him, "What do you want me to do with that thing?"

"The Officer looked puzzled. He officiously informed me that it was important physical evidence of a major crime, and as a Crime Scene Technician, it was my duty to process it and take it in to Central Property and Evidence, and log it in as such.

"Are you insane? You really think we log in human turds as evidence on a burglary?"

"He nodded.

"I *had* to play this moron; this was just too juicy to ignore. This guy was truly an idiot. How did he make it through the Academy?

""You want me to dust it for prints?"

"Again, he nodded, all wide-eyed and excited. What the hell were they *teaching* these little rat bastards in the Academy these days?

"Sure, why not? We can take some photos, dust it for possible latent prints, weigh it, take its temperature, collect a small sample for DNA, and run it through IBIS, too, for ballistics comparison.

"Assholes have lands and grooves, too, just like gun barrels, and human turds are often matched up with their owners because of their unique distinguishing characteristics. We solve a lot of cases that way."

"The officer was taking it all in, with rapt attention. I was surprised he wasn't writing all this bullshit down in his notebook.

"The kid was ecstatic, you'd have thought we'd just solved the JFK assassination. This goof was definitely a candidate for the F.B.I.

"Okay, let me call our Feces Retrieval Team...they're an elite, hand-picked bunch. That's all they do, run around taking fecal samples on major crime scenes like this one. I'll have to generate some paperwork first, and I'm out of the special forms I have to fill out, so I have to go back to the Crime Lab to get some. I'll have to wrap and box it all up for transport to Washington, too, so the FBI's special Feces Lab can deal with it, too. I have some of the Federal packaging material back at the Lab, too. I'll just run back and get what I need, and get back here ASAP..."

"So, just stand by and keep this scene secured until I get back. Let your Rank know you'll be tied up a while with the FRT. We're pretty busy tonight, so it might take a while..." (Author's experience)

The Federal Bureau of Investigation was formed in 1908.

I JUST SHOT MYSELF!

"The call came out as a Signal 24 on North Dorgenois, so my partner and I went over there on a Code 2. It was just a couple of blocks away, anyway. And besides, it had been a boring shift, and I was ready for something a little different.

"The complainant came outside immediately and was at our side even before we had come to a stop. His right hand was wrapped in a blood-soaked towel, and he was pretty agitated. And we were immediately surrounded by a screaming mob of friends, relatives, and passers-by, who wanted us to fix the man or take him to an Emergency Room.

"Anyone who can run around like the guy did, wasn't in imminent danger of losing his life, so we took him to Charity after advising our rank. EMS was tied up on something else, so we were going to be it, anyway.

"We got him to Charity and escorted him in, and at that moment, he conveniently fell over on the floor. Cute. The Charity staff wasn't impressed, either...they'd seen it all, too. We set the guy down in one of the seats and awaited our turn.

"I started the paperwork as we watched over the guy. Blood slowly dripped out of his towel and pooled up on the floor. No big deal, this was West Admit, and blood here was as common as dirt. The guy moaned occasionally. We were grateful that none of his friends had showed up yet; but then, the place was awash with suffering humanity, and between the flies, the heat, the humidity, loud conversations, yells, angry arguments, crying babies, and all, it was pretty noisy. My uniform was soaked, and my partner kept mopping his face.

"We slowly pieced the story together...the guy kept his most prized possession, a nickel-plated Smith & Wesson Model 29...a huge .44 Magnum "Dirty Harry" revolver with a six and a half inch barrel, atop a shelf in his bedroom closet, so his kids couldn't get at it, but he could. He kept it loaded, in case people gave him trouble or broke in.

"A friend of his had come over, and they had spent a nice evening together, smoking and drinking and telling tall tales as they hushed everyone else. At one point, our guy was going to show off his pet hand-cannon to impress his friend, and he went to get it.

"He had reached up, felt the big gun...he couldn't *see* it...and, grabbing it by its barrel, he had pulled it out. But it had stuck on something, so he decided to just yank it out. *That...was a mistake...*

"BLAM!"

"For *no reason at all*, the gun had somehow gone off in his hand, blasting a decent-sized hole in it, and through the wall behind him. He didn't feel anmything...at first. Everyone came running into the room to see what had happened, and when his common-law had seen the hole in her man's hand, she had started screaming and flopping around and begging Jesus to send His angels to help...

"Someone had finally made the call, and we were summoned.

"Eventually, we got the guy patched up, and we even took him home. We had to help him into his place...he was so drugged up, he could barely walk.

"We found out that it had all been an accident. The common-law wife had screwed something into the shelf in the closet, and she didn't realize that the screws were too long for the job. It was too tall for her to see. Anyway, the head of one of the screws had apparently protruded through the trigger guard and came to rest a short distance from the revolver's trigger. When the guy had yanked on the revolver by the barrel, well, you know what happened next. A neat booby trap.

"The gun had been turned in by the common-law, run through MOTION, and came up stolen, so it was taken into police custody for return to its rightful owner. But the rank decided not to charge the guy, his blown apart hand was deemed punishment enough. Things were a *lot* different in those days..." (Police Officer)

> *This guy got shot trying to pull a 64-G (armed robbery with a gun) on Royal Street, in the French Quarter. His 'victim' turned the tables on him and shot him three times with his own gun! What amused me was that the guy had the remains of his last meal...a spaghetti dinner...oozing from a gaping wound in his shoulder..." (Police Officer)*

MR. BILL

"I used to work with a real character...an older guy. We called him 'Mr. Bill.' He was divorced, but he still loved his wife. He didn't think much of me, though. 'Mr. Bill' used to smoke those cheap mule turd cigars... God, how I hated those things. Of course, the more I objected to his trying to asphyxiate me with his stinking cigar smoke, the more it encouraged him.

"Later on, he switched to a pipe. After those cigars, I actually *enjoyed* the pipe. 'Mr. Bill' was old-fashioned and a soft touch...the kids on our beat knew they could get away with almost anything. Of course, back in those days, kids were a lot different than they are now.

"Anyway, 'Mr. Bill'...with his white hair, he looked like a tough Santa. The kids loved him. He'd buy them snowballs and candy. They reciprocated wtih their little gifts and tribute. Bill would let them sit in the police car. Once in a while, he'd let one of them turn on the siren.

"Bill had a bad ticker, but that didn't do much to stop him from indulging in his two vices...smoking and drinking. He'd tell me, "Hell's bells, boy, those goddamed doctors don't know so much!", and he'd light up another cigar.

"Mr. Bill' loved old whiskey, but he'd suck on brandy, too. He'd even carry a little silver flask sometimes, to take a nip now and then, in the winter. He never got drunk, or even tipsy. I caught him with brandy in the flask sometimes. I'd laugh at him.

"'Mr. Bill' hated the French. I called his brandy a 'French faggot drink'...that used to burn him up, which I thought was really funny, considering his last name and all.

"Bill was crazy about old things. Old crystal, for instance. He used to tell me that if he had all the money he wanted, he'd buy lead crystal decanters and fill them with his favorite whiskey and Cognac and brandy. He wanted to have them set out in a big oak-panelled room, with shelves of old leather books lining the walls.

"He wanted a big gun cabinet, too, with dark wood , but lined with green velvet ("Like a billiard table," he'd tell me) and a light bulb in top to shine on his gun collection. 'Mr. Bill' had a lot of old guns, including an English double rifle, I think it was a 'Westly-Richards,' that fired immense brass cartridges. It was an elephant gun. He had a lot of old double-barrelled shotguns, too.

"We worked together for fourteen years on the same beat. We were partners the whole time. On his off days, 'Mr. Bill' just ceased to exist. He never seemed to go anywhere, or have any visitors, from what I could see. I knew he had had kids, but they had all grown up and moved away. I guessed he spent most of his time in his apartment reading his old books and listening to his radio set to the oldies stations.

"Mr. Bill' was a great cop. He used his brains instead of his fists. He could usually talk things over with people, and prevent a confrontation. But if you got out of hand, he could definitely wear your ass out, with his fists or his stick. He used to carry a mahogany table leg, but, normally, it was deliberately left in the car.

"Mr. Bill' was a wonderful pistol shot, too. He used to be on the department's old pistol team, but that was a long time before. He used to carry an old Smith & Wesson Model 10, in blue steel. He always kept that old revolver spotless. As a matter of fact, it was that same gun he used to kill himself with, the week after they forced him to retire..." (Name withheld)

> *Just as I shall select my ship when I am about to go on a voyage, or my house when I propose to take a residence, so I shall choose my death when I am about to depart from life."*
>
> *(Seneca)*

POLICE FARCE

"One afternoon, back in the 80s, I was picking up some repaired gear at F&B police supplies in Metairie. Suddenly, an entire police department walked in. All three of them! Some tiny agency from the North Shore.

"A 6-star Chief, a 4-star Assistant Chief, and a youngster devoid of rank. I noted that all of them shared the same last name.

They were just there to browse and enjoy the ambiance after dining at a nearby restaurant.

"And, when they left a few minutes later, the youngster went out the door proudly wearing his shiny new Captain's bars! He had been eyeing them wistfully in the display case, and was 'promoted' on the spot." (Author's experience)

There actually was a 'free lunch' at one time in this country, and it was invented here in New Orleans. The 'free lunch' was invented by M. Philippe Alvarez of the St. Louis Hotel's bar in 1837... and lasted until passage of the 18th Amendment. In case you're wondering, Antoine's is the oldest operating restaurant in New Orleans, opening for business in 1840.

THE OLD MAN

"I was on patrol and spotted this drunk driver all over the road. I really despise drunk drivers. My rule was, if the driver hit the white center line three times in the same block, he was drunk driving...and I would go after him.

"Well, this guy was a record setter. I turned on the overheads and pulled him right over...an old, skinny black man. I started right in on him...the entire riot act. He just nodded. I told him, "You're drunk driving, Mister; and, you're going to jail."

"The man kept his eyes down, looking at his shoes, and said, "Yassuh."

"I told him all sorts of stuff. All the old man did was look at his shoes and say, "Yassuh."

"I finally asked the old man if he had anything to say,

before I took him to jail.

"The old man just looked at me, right in the eye, tears running down his cheeks. He told me, "Officer...my wife is a *bitch*!"

"Now, what could I *do* with a defense like that? I felt like a misbehaving little kid in front of a beloved teacher.

"So, in the end, I helped him lock up his car, and then I carefully, respectfully, drove the old boy home..." (Deputy Sheriff)

"Kid, I know you love police work. But police work doesn't love you back..."

(Author)

FATALITY ACCIDENT

"One afternoon, "Tonka" and I received a call 'down the road' on St. Bernard Highway which turned out to be a fatality accident.

"Some innocent kid riding his bicycle was struck from behind by a drunk driver hot-rodding along at high speed in a pickup truck; the impact was so powerful, it jammed the child and his smashed bicycle deep into the truck's engine compartment.

"To complicate matters, the drunk driver lost control of his vehicle, and the truck veered off the highway and into an adjacent canal, where most of it sank in the muddy water. We called for a tow truck to get the drunk's pickup truck out of the canal. I had to attach the tow truck's hook to the back of the pickup truck so we could pull it out.

"The drunk driver was shook up, wet, muddy, but basically unhurt; he kept asking us who he could sue to replace his truck. We advised him to shut up or we'd show him what pain *really* was. One of the road deputies placed him under arrest, 'cuffed him, placed him into the transport vehicle, and, bless his heart, he made the guy *watch* as we dug the child's remains out of his pickup truck...

"When we pulled the pickup truck up out of the canal, we saw the crushed bicycle and then one of the child's feet. It was a terrible sight, that lifeless foot emerging from the mud and water...his shoe and sock had been ripped off in the tremendous impact. The drunk driver didn't seem to care, one way or the other. All *he* cared about was who would pay to replace his truck. Bastard...

"We had to tear the pickup truck's engine compartment apart to recover the child's body. A new Deputy Sheriff/EMT on the his first call with us got so upset when we were removing the child's remain...the unforgettable sounds of the child's shattered leg bones grating together unnerved him...he started throwing up as I arranged the child's remains and placed him into the body bag. The new man quit when we got back to the Sheriff's Office wash rack to clean the emergency unit. He didn't say much, he just quietly got into his car and drove away. He'd had enough.

"When my partner "Tonka" first saw the child's body, he freaked...he thought it was his son. He was *extremely* upset. I advised him to go sit in our unit in the air conditioning and just cool off while I got things sorted out. He didn't argue.

"Tonka" begged me to stop at his house on our way back to the Courthouse, so he could check on his son. When he saw that his son *was* alive and well, he broke down. Completely. I told him to just stay home for the remainder, with his son, and we managed to get his personal car back to his house later on that night. But the next day, he was back, like nothing had happened.

Good man." (Author's experience)

"No good Homicide Detective believes in coincidence..."
(Detective)

NO ACCIDENT

"We had an incident at a little black bar in Meraux some years ago. The Radio Room put out a 34-C (stabbing) call at (name deleted) Bar, so I went over there. I was seconds away. I pulled up in the bar's parking lot just as a tall black dude came flying out of the front door, bleeding like a stuck pig. He saw the Sheriff's Office unit right there on top of him, so he flopped out in the parking lot and started screaming for Jesus to save him. I had handled incidents in the bar before, so I ignored the bleeding man on the ground and got my riot gun.

"The guy on the ground was a career dope fiend, burglar and thief we knew as 'Miles the Magnificent Motherfucker.' He yelled out to me that a fat bitch named 'Tonya' had cut him. She was still inside. I heard the other units' sirens approaching, so I radioed that I was 10-97, put the Remington 870 at port arms, and entered the bar.

"The jukebox was blasting away. I jacked a fresh 12-gauge buckshot shell into the shotgun, and everything got quiet real fast. The bar's denizens knew the score. All of them got up quietly from their stools and moved over to the walls and assumed 'the position.' The bartender, known as 'Tubguts,' nodded at the woman's rest room, so I knew where Tanya was. I waited silently for my reinforcements.

"On the floor was a pile of fresh litter...a cheap little .25 automatic had been silently dropped to the floor and kicked away from its owner. There was an interesting assortment of pills, funny cigarettes, and various other substances tossed on the floor, too. I grinned.

"Suddenly, there was a tremendous "BOOM!" as a shotgun went off in the doorway. I must have jumped two feet when that thing went off.

Deputy Schultz had been a trifle careless with his Ithaca 12-gauge and had accidently blasted off a shell into the wall beside him. I glanced over at him and started laughing...

Schultz was swallowing, choking, and sneezing, covered with sheetrock dust and bits of wood paneling. Crazy bastard was the living incarnation of "Barney Fife"...

"Still laughing, I told the people to leave the bar. All but one complied. The last guy maintained a rigid spread-eagle against the wall. He was shivering, and his eyes were big as saucers. I again told him to leave, "Just go home, slick."

"You know what that cat told me?

"No, man, I ain't moving. I know how you crackers treat niggers in St. Bernard Parish, and I don't wanna be no fuckin' *accident*!" (Deputy Sheriff)

I don't know what effect these men will have upon
the enemy, but, by God, they terrify me."
(The Duke of Wellington)

BAD DOG

"We got a weird call on North Dorgenois. A '21' (complaint) involving a vicious dog. We rolled over to the address and immediately met the complainant...a little old man who looked pretty shook up. He came up to us, shaking and all nervous, and really glad to see us. He grabbed my hand and pumped it.

"He said, "Thanks for coming out so fast, Officers. You guys gotta *do* something about that dog in my yard! He just tried to bite me again! I had to go out to get some groceries, but now that dog won't let me back into my own yard!"

"As he's saying all this, he's looking back into the yard, which was surrounded by a large iron fence. The fence was all rusty. It was ancient.

"My partner and I looked into the yard.. There was no dog visible. All we could see were leaves, the lawn itself, and a few weeds. No dog. I glanced at my partner and caught his eye. We both were thinking the same thing... "*Another wacko*!"... The dog existed only in the old man's mind.

"I went over to the gate, to open it. The old man, his eyes bugged out, ran over and grabbed my arm as I opened the gate.

"Oh, no, Officer! *Please* don't go in there. He'll tear you up! *Look at his teeth*!" He pointed into the yard, at a patch of grass. I tell you, that old man had one hell of an imagination.

"I didn't see anything that looked like a dog, but I wanted

to placate the old man. I didn't want him to vapor lock on me out there or have a stroke...he was pretty worked up.

"I looked at my partner, and back at the old man. "Hey, sir, I can go in there and get that dog out for you. We have special police training. I took the NOPD Canine Course. We can take care of him for you, once and for all. He'll never bother you again." Of course, I was lying my ass off.

"Now, the old man was looking at me like *I* was the nut case. He said, "Officer, I don't want you to go in there and get all chewed up. Maybe you ought to shoot him from out here. That way I'll know he's really dead, and he'll never bite me or my wife again. Can't you just shoot him?"

"Now, I wanted to calm the old man down, but there was no way in hell I was going to start popping caps at a patch of grass. My partner at the time, a real moron, just had to start talking then.

"He said, "Sure, Cap, we'll shoot him for you. No problem with that. But we got to be careful, if anyone finds out we'll get in bad trouble. You can't ever tell anyone we shot your dog...we'd lose our jobs. But, if we shoot the dog, will you be satisfied?"

"The old man nodded vigorously. He was all enthusiastic about us shooting the damned dog. I was discreetly shaking my head, but my idiot partner had to have his fun. Sadistic bastard. I wanted to shoot *him.*

"Go ahead, Jim, you're the master shot. Bust that there dog so we can get back on the street."

"Both my asshole partner and the old man looked at me expectantly. I was going to kick my partner's ass when we cleared this call. The old man was all excited...he was about to blow a gasket. What else could I do? I was outnumbered.

"I looked slowly around. No one was visible anywhere. No one was looking out any of their windows. I slowly pulled my Smith & Wesson, a Model 66, took careful aim at the patch of grass the old man had pointed at, and carefully squeezed off a round.

"POW!"

"Then I rammed the gun back in the holster. I wanted to clear the scene before nervous folks started making complaints to the District. I looked around cautiously, I was checking to see if *anyone* had witnessed my little idiocy. Nothing moved. Everthing was exactly the same as before. Except the old man...

"He was a little skittish, but he slowly walked over and opened the gate. Carefully. He looked over at the patch of grass I'd shot, then he relaxed. He turned back to me and smiled.

"Nice shot, son. You *got* that son of a bitch! He'll never bite me again. Thank you boys so much. Let me get my wife out here to see this, she'll be so relieved you killed that black devil for us."

"The old man walked briskly up the sidewalk, climbed the steps, opened the door, and disappeared into the house.

"My partner started giggling. He said, "Good shootin', killer! That yard never had a chance! You are one helluva gunfighter!" he was laughing.

"Go pound sand up your ass," I told him.

"The old man appeared on the porch and motioned to us. He wanted us to come in.

"We walked up the sidewalk, climbed the steps, and met the old couple on the porch. The old man's wife had tears in her eyes. She came over and hugged me, which made me pretty uncomfortable.

"She kept saying, "Thank you! Thank you! You've answered my prayers! Thank God for you boys!" She couldn't stop thanking us. She was wacko, too. She offered us some iced tea, and of course my asshole partner accepted before I could stop him.

"It was quiet in the neighborhood. Even the police radio went silent. We drank our iced tea quietly. The old man came over and pressed a nasty old ten-dollar bill into my hand, but I wouldn't take it.

"No way!" I told him. "Thanks, Mister, but we can't take money for this. We just wanted to help you out, and we're glad we could do something for you nice folks. We've got to go now." I handed my glass back, and thanked the old lady for the tea.

"We turned to get off the porch, to return to our squad car. My partner said, "Glad we got rid of that bad dog for you folks...and if you need anything else, you just call us, and we'll come right over."

"The old people were nice, but stone cold nuts, and I wanted to get away from them fast.

"As we were walking down the steps, I was wondering

about where I was going to punch my partner first, when he grabbed my arm, and whispered, "*Jesus Christ! Look at that*!"

"I saw him pointing to the patch of grass I'd shot. I glanced at it and like to shit my pants. Where I'd fired into the yard...there was a pool of blood! No kidding, a big pool of blood, it must have been three or four feet across. Flies were landing in it. I shuddered.

"My partner and I looked at each other, and back at the old couple on the porch... They were smiling and waving. I told my partner, "Let's get the fuck outta here NOW!"

"I had chill-bumps all over me. We got back to our unit and drove off fast, and never, *ever* went back to that place..." (Police Officer)

"There is nothing impossible in the existence of the supernatural: its existence seems to me decidedly probable."

(George Santayana)

THAT GUY

"Funny, the things you remember. Back in the late 70's, I was employed as a Deputy Sheriff/EMT for the St. Bernard Sheriff's Office, but resided at 13,501 Chef Menteur Highway in New Orleans East.

"I was off-duty and busy with household chores in my apartment, but had my police scanner turned on while I worked. It kept me informed, and it both excited and relaxed me while I worked.

"Suddenly, my ears perked up: a NOPD 7th District team was requesting EMS on a "Heavy Code 3" for a vehicular accident about a mile and a half from my apartment. A motorcyclist had slammed into the back of a dump truck stopped in his lane, and it was a bad one, a possible fatality. No EMS units were available, so I jumped into my personal vehicle...I maintained a well-stocked trauma kit...and proceeded to the scene.

"The guy had literally flattened his face and was drowning in his own blood, but I kept him going until an ambulance arrived and took us over to Methodist Hospital's Emergency Room just a few miles away. They initiated prompt, expert medical treatment, so I asked the NOPD guys for a ride back to my car. They were glad to oblige.

"I forgot about the incident until a year or so later, when I was standing in line to pick up a take-out order at a local restaurant, and this guy ran up to me and started pumping my hand and hugging me, and thanking me profusely. HE was that guy..." (Author's Experience)

"I used to work with a guy who proudly wore his handcuffs in a belt pouch in the center of his back. He hard a time getting to them, but he suffered through that, and with wearing holes in his police cars' seats, because it looked 'symetrical' and he appreciated that. But he had no problem at all breaking his spine in a bad physical struggle on a City sidewalk with a big guy, and he finally adjusted to life in a wheelchair reasonably well..." (Police Sergeant)

CALL ME A HOOK...

"We had a couple of old deputies on the midnight shift. They were worthless. After roll call, they'd get in their unit and then vanish into their patrol slot. They never answered their radio, so we had to handle *their* calls besides our own. It pissed us off, you know?

"Now, the Captain knew all about the two old farts, but he didn't tell them anything. One night we had an incident. One of the deputies bitched at the Captain that if so-and-so and so-and-so, the old guys, had answered their own calls, there wouldn't be a problem. All of us knew that they were off sleeping somewhere, but they were canny enough to hide so we couldn't find them.

"The Captain gave me the eye. I walked over to him.

"Let's go," he said. We drove off in my marked car.

"The Captain directed me back into a section of my beat I'd never seen before. We had to drive through a wooded area to get there. I almost got stuck, but we got there anyway.

The Captain made me turn off the car lights, and then shut off the engine. "Get your jack," he told me, "and be real quiet."

"I did as the Captain instructed. He led me off into the darkness, under some thick trees.

"We *heard* the two old deputies before we saw them. Their snores were incredible. They had pulled up under a huge tree and were almost invisible in the thick brush.

"The Captain told me what to do...

"Jack up the rear of the car, so it's rear wheels are off the ground." He wanted absolute silence.

"I took the jack and got to work.

"Slowly, I got the wheels lifted off the ground. I didn't really make too much noise. It probably didn't mean much anyway. Those old guys were *really* sawing logs, you know what I mean?

"When I had finished, I went back and met the Captain. He said, "Go back to your car. Nah... stay here and watch this. You might learn something." I could see him grin.

"He got on his portable radio and informed Dispatch to change everyone to channel two.

"Dispatch told everyone to 10-99 (change channels to F-2), there was some special training on channel one. None of us had portables back then, except the Captain.

"After checking the frequency, the Captain had Dispatch start calling the car number of the two old deputies' unit...D.R.12. No answer. He made Dispatch call several times. No response from the two old deputies. *Their car radio was turned off!*

"No wonder they never heard their calls!

"Don't get excited," the Captain told me, "just watch. This is going to get interesting." He took out his Colt Detective Special and fired six quick shots into the ground...

"I took my fingers out of my ears. The old mens' snoring had stopped. We could see the deputies' heads jerking around frantically, trying to see what happened. Deputy (name withheld) got the unit started fast, I have to admit. But, when he put it into drive, it didn't go anything, but the engine roared as he stepped on the gas. They *couldn't* go anywhere with the rear wheels off the ground. I started to enjoy the situatiom.

"The Captain started yelling, "108!" into the radio. We could hear its amplified volume booming inside the car. I started laughing.

"The Captain kept yelling into his portable..."Headquarters, shots fired! 108! Shots fired! Send us EMS on a heavy 3 to this location! Send me backup on a heavy 3!" He yelled a *bunch* of stuff.

"Over the high-RPM roar of the patrol car's engine, we could hear the two old deputies' loud cursing. It was *great*!

"Finally, the Captain stopped yelling into his radio. I stopped laughing but was still enjoying this caper.

"The two old deputies never even *bothered* getting out of their car. They just sat there, cursing each other, still groggy. Deputy (name withheld) finally let off the accelerator. It got quieter.

"Then the Captain said over the radio, "Headquarters, send D.R. 12 to the scene to assist.Tell 'em to get here fast."

"Headquarters, in on the gag, started calling D.R. 12 to respond to the shooting scene. Deputy (name withheld) answered promptly. Of course, he had no idea where that was.

"One of the old deputies, not fully awake, responded, "Headquarters, this is 12. Our unit just went 10-7 (out of service). Send me a 'hook' to pick up the unit and give us a ride."

"Headquarters was quick. "10-23 (stand by), 12, give me your '20' (location) so I can send the tow truck. The Captain is coming over to give you guys a lift."

"Dead silence from the two deputies.

The Captain walked over to them and chewed their asses *thoroughly...*" (Deputy Sheriff)

"On an occasion of this kind it becomes more than a moral duty to speak one's mind. It becomes a pleasure."

(Oscar Wilde)

THE BRAWL

"I'm glad I never felt the need to enter politics. They'd have had a field day digging up dirt on me. Here's a freebie...I knocked a woman unconscious once. Yes. I damned sure did. I'd do it again, too, if the situation happened today or tomorrow.

"My partner and I were responding to a barroom brawl at a riverfront dive in Arabi, Louisiana, just a stone's throw from New Orleans.

"We arrived just in time to see an officer come bursting through the front window. It wasn't glass, but a thick sheet of Plexiglas with an attached iron grill, which indicated the place's level of cool sophistication.

"There were shouts and screams and weird noises emanating from the depths of the joint, and so my partner and I went in warily. Inside, it looked like a movie set...everything was flipped over, broken, shattered, leaking, or bleeding. Glass shards covered the floor, mixed with pig's feet, huge dill pickles, boiled eggs, and broken beer bottles.

"The heavily armored juke box had been murdered, it just sat there, dark and silent and lifeless...

"It was very dim, and the floor was slick with spilled beer, blood, and God only knows what else. Someone wearing one of our uniforms was slumped on the floor at the foot of the bar, moaning and vomiting. We couldn't recognize him, because he didn't have a face. Well, he did, but we couldn't see it...a large portion of his scalp had been torn open and the hair and bloody tissue drooped down, covering his features. He'd been scalped, more or less.

"Another one of our guys was lying on the floor, face up, but unmoving and apparently unconscious. My partner ran back to our marked unit, so he could retrieve his nightstick, which was a long mahogany table leg with a heavy brass buttcap, from the car's trunk, where he kept it hidden from our Platoon Commander and Sergeant.

"As my partner cleared the door to get back outside, the barroom brawl charged me. The guy was around six foot six and built like a pro football player, with immense shoulders and Popeye forearms. He picked up a barstool to crunch me, but I stepped sideways, sliding on the slick floor, and he lost his footing, too.

"As he slid by me, bellowing, I chopped him, very hard, just under his nose, and as he went down, I struck again, a vicious rabbit punch to the occipital region.

"To my surprise, this knocked him cold. I was glad...I never bothered with a nightstick or cosh or sap or any of that exotic stuff.

"I handcuffed the guy and made sure to double lock the cuffs, and searched him for weapons.

"To my complete shock, I discovered that 'he' was a 'she', and at that moment, my partner returned triumphantly with his table leg, but he saw me quietly handling the fallen brawler, and I told him to put out a "Code 4" for police cars but to get them to send us EMS on a Code 3...we didn't have portable radios in those days, so we had to use the unit's onboard radio.

"The timid bartender, who had hidden himself throughout the struggle, approached us just as we were departing the scene, but I flipped him off and grinned as we rolled off serenely off into the night. I'd do the report, but not at the moment..." (Police Officer)

MOTION is an acronym for Metropolitan Orleans Total Information On-line Network.

THE PARADOG

"This happened some years ago in east New Orleans, by the Green Bridge. The bridge is actually painted gray now, but for quite a while, it was bright green and everyone still calls it the 'Green Bridge.' It is a large bridge, two lanes running north and two south, with the height in the center span something like one-hundred-and-eighty feet. We've handled several suicides there over the years.

"We had dropped an assortment of objects off the 'Green Bridge' over the years...oxygen tanks, broken typewriters, 5-gallon water jugs, anything cumbersome and heavy was considered suitable for disposal from the bridge. We always dropped the stuff at night, so civilians wouldn't see what we were up to. Or our rank, of course...

"In this operation, we had to dispose of a bad dog. A German Shepherd that was temperamental and had attacked a few people. Now, you got to understand that usually we just *assassinated* dogs like that...a bullet from a .22 rifle worked wonders on them. But, for one reason or other, we had decided to execute this particular dog by other means. Somehow we decided to kill him with a low-level parachute drop...from the 'Green Bridge.'

"Of course, we actually hoped the dog would survive the drop, and in that event, he would be allowed to go free. But, if he died in the attempt, that was acceptable, too. You should realize that the four of us involved in this caper were all military or ex-military, including a Special Forces Office, two special warfare combat veterans, and a Military Police Sergeant. When we were committed to an operation, we knew we could be crippled or killed, and accepted that possibility. And the dog *had* been condemned to death...

"I had the most parachute experience, and a suitable parachute, too. A white nylon sixteen-footer, a pretty thing. My compadre, 'Crazy Al,' made the dog a harness. I improvised a deployment bag and static line from a pillow case and some nylon rope and rubber bands. I carefully packed the parachute, which would be secured to the makeshift harness with a mountain climber's carabiner.

"Finally, we were ready. The doomed German Shepherd was captured and placed in a police unit for it's ride to the drop zone. I would be the 'jumpmaster,' and 'Crazy Al' would be the static-line anchor-point, and a witness to our experiment. The 'drop zone control officer' was the Military Police sergeant, who was equipped with a .22 revolver to dispatch the dog in case of a parachute malfunction or other unforeseen event. His job was to secure the 'drop zone' from unwanted witnesses, dispatch the animal if required, and, above all else, to 'sanitize' the drop zone, taking the parachute and other incriminating evidence away.

"The grinning Special Forces Officer was an additional witness, and would be taking movies of the actual dog drop. He and the sergeant would secure the 'drop zone' and signal when it was safe to drop the poor dog. All of us would drive to the 'drop zone,' let out the 'drop zone control team,' and 'Crazy Al.' I would proceed to the top of the bridge and perform the final assembly of the dog's harness and perform the actual parachute drop.

"We ironed out the final details while en route to the Green Bridge. 'Crazy Al' drove the police car, and the Special Forces Officer sat up front with him. I sat in back with the sergeant and the doomed dog. It was cold and overcast, with a chill breeze from the north, off Lake Pontchartrain. A light drizzle. Miserable weather...perfect for clandestine operations.

"We dropped off the 'drop zone control team' and drove back atop the bridge. We would drop the German Shepherd on the north side of the Mississippi River Gulf Outlet, from the southbound lane of the bridge. In the appropriate spot, 'Crazy Al' stopped the police car and switched on the emergency flashers. I finished the final checkout of the dog's parachute, harness, and the static line and 'deployment bag.' The German Shepherd sensed he was in serious trouble. He sat quietly on the seat, gently licking my hand. 'Crazy Al' got out of the car, walked over to the side of the bridge, and looked over the side at our colleagues far below. There was no traffic to be seen anywhere.

"Getting the 'go' signal from the 'drop zone control team,'

'Crazy Al' turned and gave me a curt nod. He stepped back to the car and opened the door, grabbing the dog while I carried the parachute assembly and static line. Swiftly, I gave the end of the static line to 'Crazy Al,' who wrapped it around his right wrist and wedged himself tightly against the bridge railing. With a grin, I took the dog and parachute and threw them over the rail...

"It was an amazing sight. As he cleared the rail, the German Shepherd assumed a spread-eagle position, like a trained skydiver. He made no sound as he accelerated toward the cold ground nearly two hundred fee below. As his speed increased, his ears started to flap in the slipstream. His tail streamed behind. The dog rocketed downward, silent, in perfect position.

"The static line paid out perfectly its full length. The German Shepherd continued to accelerate. I couldn't believe how quiet it all was. In my own parachute jumps it was always so noisy, both from the aircraft engines and the wind-roar. But, this was eerily silent.

"At the end of the static line, the 'deployment bag' cracked open and the parachute suspension lines zoomed out smartly. Then the parachute's canopy unfolded swiftly, then broke loose from its apex bands in the makeshift 'deployment bag.' The German Shepherd was finally free of his attachment to us, and only the parachute could save him now...

"The parachute streamed for a while, what paratroopers call a 'cigarette roll.' Our eyes followed it down...the German Shepherd was still silent in his death-fall. Abruptly, before our unbelieving eyes, the canopy blew open with a "SNAP!" The German Shepherd was hidden from our view as the smooth white nylon blossomed open in a perfect deployment. Then we heard the German Shepherd for the first time...a weird, plaintive,

'WHOOO,' as he got his opening shock. Then the gently breathing canopy crumpled as the German Shepherd hit the ground.

"We got the deployment bag and static line secured quickly, then jumped into the police car, snapped off the overhead lights, and drove like maniacs to retrieve the 'drop zone control team.' 'Crazy Al' and I started laughing in the car at the unusual spectacle. We hoped the dog had survived his adventure. No one had seen out little operation, so it appeared to be a perfect success.

"Back at the 'drop zone,' we were greeted by the grinning sergeant and the Special Forces officer...*and* the German Shepherd! He had made a perfect ass-first landing, and appeared to be unhurt. The parachute was secured, and we freed the dog from his harness. He jumped around on the cold ground, frisky as hell, jumping up on us and licking us and barking.

"We failed in our security arrangements, however. Out on the water, a wide-eyed tugboat captain was eyeing us through his binoculars, still shaking his head in disbelief. We secured the operation and hauled ass...

"We were all glad the German Shepherd survived his ordeal. We were so impressed with his demeanor we treated him to a couple of warm hamburgers and let him go free. We still have the movies of 'The Paradog' and his amazing adventure..." (Name and Agency withheld by request)

A sense of humour keen enough to show a man his own absurdities will keep him from the commision of all sins, or nearly all, save those that are worthy committing."

(Samuel Butler)

THE N.O.P.D. SHOULDER PATCH

The N.O.P.D. shoulder patch is a replica of the Seal of the City of New Orleans. The Indian man and woman shown on the patch signify that the area's original inhabitants were Indians. The gray alligator, shown at their feet, symbolizes the local swamps and marshes. Between the Indian man and woman there is the representation of Neptune, brandishing his trident and pouring water from an urn. This is symbolic of the mighty Mississippi River, which gives life and prosperity to New Orleans.

At Neptune's head are the setting sun and its rays, and three Indian wigwams, all symbolizing Lousiana's warm climate. Atop the sun is a circle of stars...the twelve stars in the outer circle and a larger star in the center. These symbolize the thirteen original states admitted to the Union between 7 December 1787 and 29 May 1790. Cheap 'collector' versions of the patch usually have the number of stars wrong, or other minor discrepancies, particularly in regard to the alligator. Color variations are erratic, too, in the unauthorized patches.

There are twelve stars in the inner circle, too. These represent the states admitted to the Union between 4 March 1791 and 15 June 1836. There are another six stars, arranged in groups of three behind the Indian couple. These represent the six states admitted between 26 January 1837 and 9 September 1850. (From N.O.P.D.)

"Evidence is anything which helps in the identification and prosecution of the perpetrators of a crime." Taught in police academies all over America.

CHILD ABUSE

"I remember a case where a young fellow had an argument with his Grandmother over his use of a video game in preference to doing his school homework or performing household chores.

"His mother was doing a long stretch in prison; he never knew who his father was.

"Enraged, the youngster beat his Grandmother to death with an iron skillet, and then stabbed her 89 times with a butcher knife, to make sure. He left the knife embedded in her body. Then he looted her purse for money and called over two friends to play video games.

"They spent the entire afternoon playing video games and laughingly defiling the dead woman's corpse. It was just another game to them.

"Finally, they got bored and hungry, and called for a pizza. The pizza delivery guy saw the scene and freaked, mostly because the punks stiffed him for a tip. He came in and reported it, and was angry with *us*, too, because we wouldn't give him a 'reward'...

"By the way, the young men were 11, 11, and 12." (Author's experience)

Remember 'Lash Larue,' a popular cowboy movie star in the '40s and '50s? How about rock n' roll sensation Franke Ford ("Sea Cruise")? Or Mel Ott, baseball Hall of Fame member and former New York Giants player? Musician, author, Broadway actor R. Emmet Kennedy? All these gentlemen came from Gretna, Louisiana.

WOUNDED WOMAN

"Another EMS story I remember fondly involved a black woman who had been shot in the chest, point blank, with a .38 revolver. Domestic violence.

"When I got there, her skin resembled gray plastic, and she was soaked in perspiration, vomiting, and in convulsions. I sliced off her blouse and bra to examine the wound, assessed her rapidly, started her on oxygen and a saline drip, dressed the wound, and we transported her to the nearest Emergency Room. She watched me intently as I worked, and, at one point, she grabbed my arm and asked, "Am I gonna die?"

"Of course, I had no way to see inside her to gauge the severity and extent of the damage...I'm pretty good, but I don't have X-ray vision, and I knew from long experience that it's not only *what* you do, but *how* you do it, that can give the patient...and yourself...the edge. So, I just gave her a big smile, laughed, and replied, "From this? Hell no, sweetheart, you'll do fine."

"She did, too. I was relieved to see her relax and get with the program.

"Several months later, my squad was having breakfast in Arabi at the Frost Top restaurant, and a few of the regular street deputies had joined us, too. Suddenly, a black woman stormed in, ran up to me, hugged me, and kissed me hard on the lips. I was a little surprised, but you should have seen the *other* deputies' faces (laughs). Yes, it was *her*, and she just wanted to thank me..." (Author's experience)

(Author's Note: Jefferson Parish Sheriff Harry Lee is considered by many 'the best Sheriff in Louisiana.' The colorful Lee is known as the 'Chinese Cajun Cowboy' and runs a very professional, progressive organization. Harry Lee is living proof that a man can be a successful politician and still be a fine family man... and

an outstanding policeman).

MY F.T.O.

"The last time I worked with my Field Training Officer, he treated me to beignets and coffee from the Cafe du Monde. We parked behind a wharf, right there on the river, eating the beignets and enjoying the hot coffee and chickory. It was a beautiful spring evening, and the lights were just coming on. Ships and boats moved about on the river. We could see a welder's torch throwing huge showers of sparks somewhere in Algiers.

"My FTO told me, "Well, little lady, you made it. You've finally got the Academy bullshit in perspective, and you're starting to really know what it means to be the police in this city." He took another bite of his beignet, careful not to get the powdery white sugar on his baby blue uniform shirt.

"He continued, "Now, remember what I've taught you when you get out there with your new partner. Don't forget that if you fuck up, you make *me* look bad, and I just won't tolerate that. I know you were taught right. You know what to do. But, don't be too stubborn to ask questions. No one knows it all, in this business." He licked the sugar off his lips, and took another drink of the hot coffee.

"Remember the golden rule...*'Every good cop goes home to supper.'* You know what that means. Don't be an asshole with these people, and don't try to be John Wayne. Just do your job. You can still be a lady and stay feminine, you don't have to become an overbearing asshole like lots of these female officers tend to do."

"He scooped another hot beignet out of the bag. "You know, you really remind me of *me* when I started off in this job. You love the adrenaline burn, and the excitement. Well, you've got it bad now, little sister, and, unfortunately, you're as hooked on police work as the dope-fiends are on their own shit.

"You'll never get it out of your system." My FTO looked at me, right in the eye. "I've tried it myself, and it never worked. Police work takes over *everything* in your life, if you let it. I'm not talking about the Department bullshit, or off duty details. I'm talking about *real* police work. You know I used to be in Homicide. Well, little one, when I was a homicide detective, *that* was my entire life." He glanced away, looking at the showers of sparks on the West Bank.

"I've got something for you...a little present," he told me. He reached under the seat and pulled out a manila envelope. "Here," he told me, as he put the envelope in my hand. "I don't give one of these to *all* my people...just the *special* ones like you."

"I took the envelope, opened it, and slid out an eight by ten color photograph. It was horrible...a picture of a dead man...decomposing into a floor. He had turned colors, mostly dark brown at the hands and feet...his feet were almost black. His skin had bubbled up in places, peeling off, and fluids leaked out of him and run out onto the floor. There was a softball-sized clump of maggots where his face had been. Not very nice to look at... I didn't want any more beignets.

"Not very pretty, is he?" asked my FTO, keeping his eyes fixed across the river. "He was thirty-eight years old. He lived alone. He was dead a week before the neighbors called us about the smell. He'd been married once, and had two daughters. He was a detective, too, a damned good cop, just like you are. Like you're going to be. And...he was my partner a few years ago. He loved the job, and it became his whole life. The trouble with police work is that it's a jealous bitch. It wants everything you've got...and it gets it, too, if you let it.

"My FTO looked me right in the eye. "Little sister, you make certain we don't find *you* on a floor one of these days." (Detective Sergeant)

The New Orleans Police Department became the first police department in the United States to have two FBI Special Agents assigned to it in 1995 to investigation complaints of police corruption.

THE HOLE-IN-THE-WALL BURGLAR

"I was assigned to handle a crime scene at one of those little corner groceries uptown. The grocery had a feisty Vietnamese owner, and it occupied about a quarter of a two story apartment building, with a tiny washateria close by. This was a business burglary, and a bored patrolman was taking the report while the Vietnamese guy was yelling at anyone within earshot. Inside, I was laughing...*nothing changes much with these guys...*

"When I walked in with my camera bag and the fingerprint box, the officer brightened up, glanced at his watch, and jotted down my arrival time on his notepad. He started filling me in on the details of the burglary, and what he wanted me to do.

"The store owner maintained a small storeroom in the back of the store, and he had discovered that some of his stock was missing. Mostly boxes of cigarettes...each box contained a number of cartons, and they were very valuable. The owner was puzzled...how could anyone get back there and steal his cigarettes? There was no window, no door...no way in. It was impossible!

"I went in and looked around. Boxes were piled high against the back wall...yes, it was a pretty well-stocked storeroom. I asked the owner if I could poke around in the storeroom, with the other officer's help. He agreed readily, and I asked the patrolman to help me move some of the boxes away from the wall. He did so, grudgingly...

"As we moved boxes, it soon became apparent how the burglar had gotten in...there was a rough-hewn hole in the back wall, leading into the apartment next door. The patrolman's eyes brightened up as we uncovered the hole. *This was going to be easy!*

"The patrolman ran off to find the apartment manager, and she gave us permission to enter the room and take pictures or whatever we needed to do...no warrant necessary. The room's occupant was a young guy with a crappy attitude and he had a difficult time paying his rent on time, anyway.

"When the apartment manager finally saw the raggedy hole in her wall, she went *off,* her voice thundering, and that brought the Vietnamese guy in through the hole in the wall, and in moments, both of them were yelling and pointing and raising a ruckus. It was a real comedy.

"As all this is going on, the room's renter came in and started screaming and raising a ruckus, too...he claimed that we had broken in and were planting things in his room, and someone else was involved, you can imagine the bullshit he started spouting. And, we could all see the package of cigarettes in his pocket...the same brand that had been stolen. The Vietnamese guy ran over and started beating the crap out of the burglar...

"As the tumult continued...and escalated, I just quietly took the photos I needed, gathered what else I needed,. and let the patrolman handle the rest. *I* was done...finished. That was my last assignment with the Crime Scene Unit...and the New Orleans Police Department." (Author's experience)

N.B. The burglar covered his deeds by using a wide nylon strap...he tossed what he wanted through the hole he had made, and wrapped the strap around a pile of boxes, drawing the free ends with him as he crawled back through the hole into his room. He arranged the boxes carefully in place, and pulled them in tight with the strap, so no gap would show and reveal his hole. Then, he just pulled in one end of the strap until it was all inside with him. Simple and effective.

EPILOGUE

I've wanted to update this book since 1996, shortly after it was published. So much has changed. And not much for the better...

Currahee! From the Cherokee phrase and term, "We stand alone...together." Paratroopers were quick to adopt the word and the philosophy it represents. And so did many cops...

When I came on the job, almost everyone carried Colt or Smith & Wesson revolvers as their primary sidearms. Many of these revolvers had ornate, oversized wooden grips, some of them festooned with elaborate gold filagree buttcaps incorporating the officers' initials, badge numbers, and the like. They were meant for show, while the more serious working cops went for Pachmayr-style rubber grips.

Often, we were issued (or had to purchase) low power 'police ammunition' utilizing 158-grain round-nose lead bullets, which we saw was spectacularly ineffective on the street, particularly against armed, violent dopefiends.

Leather gear dominated the police field in those times, and

many officers used low-slung 'swivel holsters', ammunition dump pouches, and cowboy-style cartridge belts. Officers still used crossdraw suicide rigs and clamshell spring-open holsters, and some belt rigs even featured "Sam Browne" shoulder straps, because they were 'traditional'...and none of these holsters had any thought as to weapon retention or safety concerns; many of them used simple leather snap straps and had exposed trigger guards!

Instead of PR-24 and ASP batons, we carried polished hardwood table legs with brass caps for impact weapons, and some of us carried sap gloves or 'convoys' and slap jacks. No one carried aerosol sprays or stun guns in those days...they hadn't been invented yet.

Body armor wasn't used, except by highly specialised tactical units or guys assigned to the armed robbery details. It was heavy, cumbersome, hot, uncomfortable, and ineffective.

Almost no one had a portable radio; we used the Motorola or General Electric radios in our patrol units, and they were usually low-band VHF or UHF transceivers. Even the great NOPD used just a dozen UHF channels in their system.

Computers in police cars were still the stuff of science fiction.

I remember carrying three Pagers at one time: one issued by the Department for official business, my private pager for friends and family, and one I maintained just for my confidential informants. I had to carry pocketfuls of change and had to locate working telephones in the areas I worked, so that I could stay in touch. Later one, cellular telephones were invented, and I bought one. It was immense, by today's standards, and it weighed something like fifteen pounds, with its lead acid battery. Mine was a portable, and it was incredibly useful, because I was always out on the street, and was no longer restrained by land lines.

And, later on, when practical portable computers were invented and put into use, I indulged myself. I finally bought one that had a built-in printer! So, in my car, I could write up incident and supplemental reports, arrest warrants, search & seizure paperwork, you name it. My 'office' had four wheels.

I got an account with West's, so I always had them mail me the most current copy of their "West's Louisiana Statutory Criminal Law & Procedure", the same law book the Judges and District Attorneys referred to. It was worth its weight in gold, as far as I was concerned. How can one enforce the law, if one doesn't know what the law is?

Many agencies used red emergency lights. The NOPD preferred blue lights, as did the Feds. I remember a war story from when the Jefferson Parish Sheriff's Office...red light boys...intervened in a pursuit because the pursuit unit, which was unmarked, was using a blue 'Kojack' rotating dashboard light, which wasn't recognized as 'official' by the JPSO. The bad guys being chased by the U.S. Customs Special Agents in the unmarked unit escaped unscathed, and there was a heated exchange on the side of the road, between JPSO Deputies and Customs Agents, as you might imagine.

We also used 'rollover sirens' which could be heard for miles at night, when it was quiet, and they drew so much current, the headlights dimmed when they were used. Only later were the electronic sirens developed and came into widespread use in the field.

It should be noted that when I wrote THE REAL POLICE

in 1996, no female New Orleans police officer had ever lost her life in the line of duty.

That changed on Monday, August 9, 2004, when Police Officer LaToya Nicole Johnson, Badge 1261, a three year veteran, was murdered while serving commitment papers. Her murderer shot her repeatedly with a .50 pistol and was killed in a gun battle with her partner and responding officers.

And on Monday, January 28, 2008, Officer Nicola Diane Cotton, Badge 1869, a two year veteran, working alone, attempted to arrest a male subject twice her size. In the ensuing struggle, the male subject overpowered Cotton, struck her with her own defensive baton, and then gained control of her duty weapon, shooting her fifteen times. Witnesses observed the struggle for several minutes and did nothing whatsoever to assist Officer Cotton. Responding Officers took her murderer into custody without further incident, because he was out of ammunition. Officer Cotton was eight weeks pregnant at the time of her death.

On Tuesday, June 7, 2016, Police Officer Natasha Maria Hunter, Badge 686, an eleven year veteran, died of injuries she had received two days earlier when she was struck by an 'impaired driver' while assisting another officer at an accident scene on Interstate 10 near the Esplanade Avenue Exit. She was the mother of a five year old daughter. And Hunter's two sisters also serve in law enforcement. And, even as I write this, local newspapers are carrying stories about her killer trying to cut a deal with officials, hoping to negotiate a 'more lenient' sentence.

The horrors of Hurricane Katrina in August of 2005 could easily fill a hundred books. At one point, I desperately wanted to write a book dedicated to Katrina and its effects on metro law enforcement personnel and their families, but the events were too raw, and too painful, for me to explore such a book at that time. So, others will have to tell those stories in their own ways. I do not envy them.

THE REAL POLICE 'took off' surprisingly well in the New Orleans metro area, which amazed me. The initial print run of 500 copies sold out in just over two months; the second run of 1,000 copies, was disappearing rapidly until August of 2005, when Hurricane Katrina paid her fateful visit.

THE REAL POLICE was so well regarded by my bosses at the New Orleans Police Department that I was quietly, but firmly, 'encouraged' to continue my law enforcement career elsewhere. And, another factor, which I did not become aware of until I had left the NOPD, was that 'someone' had informed my bosses there that I was some kind of federal 'rat' planted on them, to get the goods on crooked cops and their nefarious schemes, and so on. That was far from the truth, but the damage was done, regardless. Now, it just makes me grin.

This is not as far fetched as it sounds, in 1995, the FBI assigned two Special Agents to the NOPD's Internal Affairs Unit, to root out corruption, civil rights abuses, and the like. That had never been done before to an American police department.

This was also the era of Len Davis and Antoinette Frank; many NOPD officers were suspected of criminal acts, and often, these suspicions eventually resulted in criminal indictments, prosecution, and convictions.

But many of us still bitterly remember Mayor Sidney Barthelemy's demand for "quantity not quality" in the NOPD's ranks...a policy that elicited harsh responses at many levels of the NOPD's rank and file, who knew the awful effects such a policy would have.

Things have steadily grown more dismal for the New Orleans Police Department and the decent people of New Orleans. Saddled with the impractical, politically-correct, agenda-driven Federal Consent Decree, and the taxpayer-funded, ultra-liberal, vehemently anti-police "Independent Police Monitor" lynch squad, and the racist, agenda-driven, illegal dictates of Mayor Mitch Landrieu, the City of New Orleans is now referred to as the Murder Capitol of America. The Chocolate City is melting...

At one point during this period of upheaval, I received death threats because I had published THE REAL POLICE, which I found rather amusing. Not bad, when you understand that I was just an anonymous, working street cop with no political aspirations, and no axe to grind; I was selling my book by word of mouth and at local police departments, gun shows, police seminars, book fairs, trade shows, and via a modest internet presence. But some people considered me a sinister menace...

And, at the time, I was working on two other books simultaneously when Katrina struck: METAL DETECTING FOR THE CRIME SCENE INVESTIGATOR, which is self-explanatory, and EVERLASTING GLORY, which dealt with famous, and some, not so famous, heroic military 'last stands' throughout history. Years of tedious collection of maps, charts, photographs, endless periods of scholarly research, correspondence, writing, polishing, re-writing...all destroyed in a few hours' time, by Katrina...

One of the fascinating little tidbits I discovered during my research was that at the infamous Alamo siege of 1836, many of the Mexican troops were armed with worn-out, obsolete firearms which they had bought from the British as war surplus!

C'est la vie.

These days, law enforcement Officers in America are working in an intensely hostile environment. A recent presidential administration was viciously and smugly hostile to law enforcement. It openly sided with violent criminals and with anti-police groups bent on murdering police officers and their families. I see no cessation in sight. Terrorist organizations in the USA flourish and, even, are given official recognition.

I was heartbroken to see that so many of the officers, colleagues, and friends I paid tribute to in the ACKNOWLEDGEMENT section, sadly, have passed away. So, in a small way, this book is a memorial...a tribute...to those fine people and their deeds and exploits. They did not live...or die...in vain.

This updated republishing of THE REAL POLICE would simply not have happened without the advice and steady encouragement of my law enforcement brother, Sergeant Roger C. Bull, JPSO (retired), and Southern Oaks Publishing, LLC, who provided expert and professional advice and support.

And a special thank you to Dea Meyers for her kind permission to use the badge graphic on the cover. It is a copyright-protected property of her Hero. Ops. LLC.

Many thanks, also, to Sgt. Warren V. Pope, NOPD (Retired), Mark Zehring, Fran Thomas, Connie Zimmermann, Yuvonda Wells, the Eichakers, Fred Yorsch, Samuel Fondren, Rob and Meredith Roy, Sidney Garaudy, John Joseph Leal, Jr., Bill Nourse, Walter Dees, Robert Spahr, Pat Thomason, Lee Guifoyle, Lila Deblanc, Nelly Chabanais, Mark Michaud, Debbie

Piantanida, Steven Rice Junior, Margaret Collier Furry, Dan Lyons, Toni Hall, Ryan M. Landry, Hillary Arnone, Cherié Wilkerson-Gilley, Ray Solis, Wade Daniels, Denise Margo Riley, Sue Eagan, Alice Brown Smith, Yvonne Eichman, Robert Caire, Cort Schaumburg, Dathi O'Briain, MJ Ruadh, Shawn Cronan, Ed Hauptmann, Michael Harrison, Debbie Vincent, SK Blank, and many others, including my good friends at Gold Coast Skydivers in Lumberton, Mississippi.

Dianna, my wife, took the photograph of me which adorns the back cover of the original book. Dianna was murdered by a drunk driver on the morning of Sunday, April 24th, 2005, while she was driving to her assignment at the East Bank Lockup of the Jefferson Parish Sheriff's Office. She took so much with her...

The color photographs on this edition's back cover include a 'selfie' I took on my last day as a policeman; the 'radio picture' was taken by Kathy Eichaker, and the 'special operations' photo was taken by Sue Eagan at Gold Coast Skydivers in Lumberton, Mississippi (now closed).

I finally turned in my police badge on July 9th, 2010, and left law enforcement forever. In the end, for me, the total cost of participating in police work was everything that mattered.

To my brothers and sisters of the badge that still carry on, I wish you and yours the very best and great success in your professional endeavors. And I hope you know when to finally let it go.

James S. Prine
Hammond, Louisiana
2017

GLOSSARY

ACP: Automatic Colt Pistol, as in, "This is a .45 ACP cartridge."
ABD: An 'abdominal' pad, utilized for major wounds.
BEIGNETS: Pillow-shaped doughnuts, coated with powdered sugar and served hot.
BERETTA: World's oldest firearms manufacturer.
BLOW GROCERIES: Energetic vomiting.
BP: Blood pressure.
CHARITY HOSPITAL: Renamed the 'Medical Center of Louisiana,' we still call it Charity.
CLU: Central Lockup, where New Orleans' prisoners are booked.
CTS: Crisis Transportation Service, a citizen volunteer unit working for the NOPD.
DEFECTIVE: Derogatory term for a detective.
DIU: District Investigative Unit
DOME: To shoot in the head. Or a reference to the Louisiana Superdome.
EMS: Emergency Medical Service.
EMT: Emergency Medical Technician.
ER: Emergency Room.
FBI: Federal Bureau of Investigation; an obscure law enforcement entity.
FLIP OUT or GO OFF: To suddenly act bizarrely or violently.
FTO: Field Training Officer.
GOA: Gone On Arrival.
HOOK: A tow truck.
HOT WATER HEATER: A water heater. (Why *heat* hot water?)
JPCC: Jefferson Parish Correctional Center.
JPSO: Jefferson Parish Sheriff's Office.
LSP: Louisiana State Police.
MAKE GROCERIES: To shop or go shopping.

MODULE: A term for a 'modular' type ambulance or emergency unit.

M.O.T.I.O.N.: Acronym for 'Metropolitan Orleans Total Information On-Line Network.'

NAT: Necessary Action Taken.

NCIC: Nationa Crime Information Center.

NCOA: No Complainant On Arrival.

NOFD: New Orleans Fire Department.

NOPD: New Orleans Police Department.

NTI: 'Nothing to It;' a 'bullshit' call.

OLB: Orleans Levee Board, also known as the Orleans Levee District.

POST: Post Mortem, an Autopsy.

RTF: Report To Follow.

S&W: Smith & Wesson, a manufacturer of high quality firearms.

SCOOP: Capture or arrest.

SCUBA: Self-Contained Underwater Breathing Apparatus.

SLIM-JIM: A tool used to open a vehicle's locked door.

THREE-PIECE POLICE: An FBI Special Agent.

UNFOUNDED: A 'bullshit' call.

UNIFORM: A detective's term for uniformed personnel.

VICAP: Violent Criminal Apprehension Program.

ZINK: New Orleans term for 'sink' or wash basin. A holdover from 'Zinc' basins.

"Headquarters, "209 10-7." "10-4, 209."

Books by James S. Prine

The Real Police: Stories from the Crescent City

Tales from the Id

75986014R00129

Made in the USA
Columbia, SC
30 August 2017